The New York Times

REAL SIMPLE CROSSWORDS

The New York Times

REAL SIMPLE CROSSWORDS
Easy, Enjoyable Puzzles

Edited by Will Shortz

ST. MARTIN'S GRIFFIN ☙ NEW YORK

ACROSS
1 Up to the task
5 Machinist's tool
10 Study all night, say
14 Common cause of postponement
15 Rural units
16 Olympic swimmer's assignment
17 Regis Philbin and others
20 Hive occupant
21 Ariz. neighbor
22 Actor Milo
23 Actress Farrow
24 Foal's mother
26 Motion picture academy honor
33 Tureen accessory
34 Hands (out)
35 Wall St. deal
36 Mystery writer ___ Stanley Gardner
37 "See? . . . huh, huh?"
38 Emptiness
39 Get older
40 Gift recipient
41 Lemon peels, e.g.
42 Alumni
45 Toward shelter
46 Passé
47 Beauty's counterpart
50 The Beatles, e.g.
52 ___ Na Na
55 There's one in 17-, 26- and 42-Across
59 Gen. Robert ___
60 Alaskan native
61 Transnational currency
62 Wines to serve with beef
63 Singer Turner and others
64 Comic Sandler

DOWN
1 ___-Israeli relations
2 Sweetie pie
3 Head case?
4 Finale
5 Nonprofessional
6 Part of a French play
7 Cereal "for kids"
8 Haw's partner
9 Language suffix
10 Place for hangers
11 Impetuous
12 A few chips, say, in poker
13 Tableland
18 Japanese cartoon style
19 Jewish circle dances
23 French miss: Abbr.
24 Setting
25 Working without ___
26 North Dakota's largest city
27 Slacker
28 Danish birthplace of Hans Christian Andersen
29 Sacred choral work
30 Irving Berlin's "When ___ You"
31 Back-of-newspaper section
32 Nonverbal O.K.'s
33 Bit of foliage
37 Reason for an R rating
38 Sell
40 Airline once said to be "ready when you are"
41 Nintendo's The Legend of ___
43 Pulverizes
44 Dunkable treats
47 1930's boxing champ Max
48 Vogue competitor
49 Mimicked
50 Square in the first column of bingo
51 Water
52 Simple earring
53 Zeus' wife
54 Molecule part
56 Flier in a cave
57 ___ Lilly, maker of Prozac
58 Actor Stephen of "The Crying Game"

by Adam G. Perl

2

ACROSS

1 Wounds with a grenade, in slang
6 ___ carte
9 Just squeeze by
13 "The Bathers" painter
15 Naked Pooh?
17 "An Inconvenient Truth" presenter
18 Sources of free drinks
19 Bullwinkle's salon application?
21 Abbr. after many a major's name
22 Lop-___
23 Opposite SSW
24 Blue
26 Omaha Beach time
27 Hollywood's Alan and Diane
29 Country's McEntire
32 Luau fare
33 Think the world of
35 Hunk
38 The Bruins' #4
39 USA Today chart shape
40 ___ Irvin, classic cartoonist
41 Washed away
43 Aardvark's morsel
44 "Beowulf" quaff
45 "___ bleu!"
48 P. & L. statement preparers
52 ___ judicata
54 Anonymous John
55 Struck down
56 Sphere in space
58 Quick Draw McGraw with laryngitis?
61 Laconic president
63 Many a realty deal
64 Bugs Bunny's coat?
65 Indigent one
66 Black cat, to some
67 Hails from Rocky
68 Reporters

DOWN

1 Set up for a fall
2 Prepare for another shot
3 Silky-coated cat
4 Loosey-___
5 Begot
6 Be plentiful
7 Ran out
8 Bellicose god
9 Fall back
10 Beloved Bambi?
11 "___ Saint-Lazare" (Manet painting)
12 Once, old-style
14 Sleep acronym
16 Hydrocarbon suffixes
20 Being broadcast
25 Oils, busts, etc.
27 Some members of Parliament
28 Left Bank locale
30 Domesticated insect
31 Org. with a noted journal
32 Creator of the Ushers
34 Get firm
35 Ring insert
36 It needs refinement
37 Porky Pig's home movie presentation?
39 Cuts back
42 1950's political inits.
46 Slow, on a score
47 Tools for apples
48 Ninth-inning pitcher
49 Main Street event, maybe
50 Market areas
51 Villainous looks
53 ___ Tzu
55 Shorn animals
56 Twice cuatro
57 Gad about
59 Anita of jazz
60 West ender?
62 Grid great Dawson

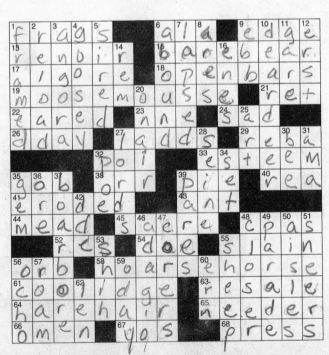

by C. W. Stewart

3

ACROSS

1 Indian chief
6 Spilling point
10 Wild ___
14 Without help
15 Mystique
16 Exploits
17 Unsuccessful batter's intro?
20 It can take your breath away
21 ___ Spiegel magazine
22 Sizes up or down?
23 Koh-i-___ diamond
25 "Waterloo" quartet
26 Hot dog vendor's intro?
33 Spiritual leaders
34 Letters on Challenger
35 Nefariousness
36 Blazing gun
37 Belt-attachable device
39 Nicknamed
40 Clouds (up)
42 Work ___ sweat
43 Assign, as the blame
45 Guard's intro?
49 Is bedridden
50 Cow-headed goddess
51 Rough-cut
54 Start and end of the Three Musketeers' motto
55 Pinnacle
59 Quotation citer's intro?
62 Lose strength in the backstretch
63 Tent event
64 Hazardous
65 Regarded guardedly
66 Biblical plot
67 Pays (up)

DOWN

1 Outdoor event planner's worry
2 A chorus line
3 ___ stick (incense)
4 Reception aid
5 Part of H.M.S.
6 Napoleon's place
7 Regretful one
8 Audit grp.
9 "Goldilocks" figure
10 Dropped movie scene
11 "But, ___ was ambitious, I slew him": Brutus
12 Eye drop
13 Retired fliers
18 Hero type
19 Napoleon's place, once
24 Green-lights
25 Notre Dame niche
26 More and more of news shows nowadays
27 Stubble remover
28 Baja buddy
29 Dearie
30 Former Mrs. Trump
31 Olympus competitor
32 Sweat ___
37 "Don't give me that!"
38 Knuckle draggers
41 Hurt
43 23rd in a series
44 "That just shouldn't happen"
46 "Peace on earth," e.g.
47 ___ Collins, former space shuttle commander
48 Tropical escape
51 Tea for two place
52 Anthem opener
53 Second
54 Fit
56 Playbill info
57 Karaoke need
58 Häagen-Dazs alternative
60 Sorry
61 Piece-keeping grp.?

by Manny Nosowsky

4

ACROSS

1 Madrid museum
6 Wear at the edges
10 Radio switch
14 Break of day
15 Wrestling ring encloser
16 Shopaholic's delight
17 Words of admiration ___ NOT!
20 Hang around
21 Architectural molding
22 Bookish sort, slangily
23 Trucker on the air
25 Shea squad
26 Company whose name is pig Latin for an insect
28 Hearth refuse
31 Item with a concave head
34 Like this clue's answer, in five letters
35 Factory whistle time
36 ___ brat
37 Words of apology ___ NOT!
40 Slippery swimmers
41 Seas of France
42 Neuters
43 Plus-or-minus fig.
44 Dated
45 Classic street liners
46 Managed care grps.
48 Creole vegetable
50 New driver, frequently
51 Fabled race loser
53 Final Four org.
57 Words of congratulation ___ NOT!
60 Tuckered out
61 Boxer's annoyance
62 Ladies' men
63 Cultural doings
64 Burg
65 Popular theater name

DOWN

1 Pitchfork-shaped letters
2 Reddish-brown
3 Tolstoy's Karenina
4 "O.K., back to work"
5 Make a choice
6 Frankincense and myrrh, but not gold
7 Memorization
8 Area that may have stained glass
9 "Uh-huh"
10 Racecourse since 1711
11 Hardly revolutionary
12 A lot of beef?
13 Funnyman Brooks
18 Tiller's tool
19 Lady bighorns
24 Memory unit
25 Selection screen
26 They're carried by people in masks
27 Pull off a high-risk feat
29 Goes bad
30 Company publication
32 TV trophies
33 Centers, of sorts
34 ___' Pea
36 According to schedule
38 Short holiday?
39 PC person
44 Early video game
47 Gymnastics competitions
49 Something under the counter that puts people under the table
50 Level
51 Hawaii's ___ Bay
52 From the top
54 French film
55 Camera setting
56 Part of P.G.A.: Abbr.
57 Eddie Gottlieb Trophy org.
58 Commonly
59 Prima donna's problem

by Nancy Salomon

ACROSS

1 Dogie catcher
6 What a tout may tout
10 Cheese in a mousetrap, e.g.
14 Road runners
15 Uncommon
16 ___ Domini
17 Rage
18 Fedora feature
19 James of TV's "Las Vegas"
20 Racehorse, slangily
21 Sweater selection?
24 Versifier
25 Mal de mer symptom
26 Shrek's lady, e.g.
29 Exams for would-be attys.
31 Feudal tribunal?
33 Tennis umpire's call
36 Aids in storming castle gates
37 It's put in an env.
38 Prefix with space
39 Wonderment
40 Bow with a price tag?
44 Secretly run off together
45 Sent to the canvas
46 Defeat in a footrace
49 Brother of Cain and Abel
50 Was familiar with a summertime allergen?
53 "Many years ___ . . ."
56 It follows a curtain's rise
57 Ancient Andean
58 No longer dirt
60 Ball in a sewing room
61 Beam with a 90 degree bend

62 Bacteria in an outbreak
63 Healthful resorts
64 Cloth measure
65 Taste or touch

DOWN

1 Homeowner's pride
2 Distinctive atmosphere
3 Guys-only
4 Boozer
5 Wisconsin city on Lake Winnebago
6 All the way around
7 Feathered missile
8 What icicles do
9 Advanced study group
10 Jim of "Gilligan's Island"
11 Diarist Nin
12 Cockamamie
13 Island nation east of Fiji
22 Home of straw, maybe
23 Women's suffrage leader Carrie Chapman ___
24 Coatrack parts
26 Gumbo vegetable
27 Bite like a beaver
28 Frost
29 Singer Lenya
30 Catch waves
32 Hoofbeat
33 Faucet fault
34 Writer ___ Stanley Gardner
35 Pigeon-___
38 Polish-born author Sholem
40 Supermodel Heidi

41 Greaseless
42 Old-fashioned music halls
43 Fixes, as a report
44 Field marshal Rommel and others
46 Gives the go-ahead
47 Open, as a toothpaste tube
48 Prefix with fluoride
49 Bit of shattered glass
51 Los Angeles Sparks' org.
52 Neighbor of Tenn.
53 Bell-ringing company
54 Breast implant materials
55 Comics dog
59 One-spot

by Sarah Keller

ACROSS

1 Cry after "Forward!"
6 Solder
10 Belgrade native
14 Central Florida city
15 Words of understanding
16 Peter, Paul and Mary, e.g.
17 Holiday decoration
20 Retain
21 Numbered work of a composer
22 "Come in!"
23 Preservers of preserves
25 "This looks bad!"
27 Cleopatra's lover
30 Hissy fit
31 Air blower
34 Like a pitcher's perfect game
35 Flub
36 Look into a crystal ball
37 Holiday decoration
40 Fabric fuzz
41 Memo opener
42 Plural of 21-Across
43 U-turn from WSW
44 Assns.
45 Frigate or ferry
46 Fleeting trace
47 Neat
48 Offspring
51 Butcher's cut
53 Shopping place
57 Holiday decoration
60 Abbr. before a colon
61 Feed the kitty
62 Make amends
63 General emotional state
64 Some boxing decisions, briefly
65 Snapshot

DOWN

1 Make fun of
2 Liniment target
3 Like one in a million
4 Business that routinely overcharges
5 Possesses
6 Ones likely to chicken out
7 Biblical pottage purchaser
8 First chapter in a primer
9 Morning moisture
10 Shorthand pro
11 The "E" in Q.E.D.
12 Baptism or bar mitzvah
13 Danish Nobelist Niels
18 British Conservative
19 What homeowners don't have to pay
24 1998 animated bug film
26 Player of 45's
27 Site for a monitoring bracelet, maybe
28 Hopeless, as a situation
29 Feudal landholder
30 Whiskey drinks
31 Confronts
32 Sky-blue
33 View from Mount Everest
35 Ship-to-shore accessway
36 Insect whose larvae destroy foliage
38 Broadcasts
39 ___ the line (behaved)
44 Pig's sound
45 Handful for Tarzan
46 Coiled
47 Multiplied by
48 Pillow cover
49 Famed Roman censor
50 Diggin'
52 "___ be in England": Browning
54 Suffix with buck
55 Long, angry discourse
56 Lt. Kojak
58 Krazy ___ of the comics
59 Doze

by Donna Levin

ACROSS

1 Slap on
5 ___ Kadiddlehopper, old TV hayseed
9 Losing rolls
14 Mont Blanc, e.g., locally
15 Classic theater name
16 Cousin of a cockatoo
17 Sign above a Tijuana A.T.M.?
20 2004 Will Smith thriller
21 Solver's cry
22 Campsite hookup user
23 "Oh Boy! What ___" (1920's hit)
25 One listed on MySpace
27 "Why did the chicken cross the road?," e.g., in Tijuana?
31 "Excuse me . . ."
32 Letters before Choice or Prime
33 Web-footed mammal
36 Plastered
37 Pick up on
38 Co. informally known as Brown
40 Charlottesville sch.
41 Israel's Dayan
43 Brontë heroine
45 QB Tarkenton
46 Tijuana air freshener?
49 Morning hour
51 Japanese cartoon genre
52 Spot for a nap
53 Biblical verb ending
55 He did not beware the Ides of March

59 Advice regarding a good poker hand in Tijuana?
62 Hoops coach Thomas
63 Crowd sound
64 Kind of clef
65 Brings in
66 Yorkshire river
67 Cry out for

DOWN

1 Painter of dreamscapes
2 Controversial spray
3 As many as
4 Plant yielding a fragrant oil
5 Point out the pluses and minuses of
6 Enter, as a record
7 Blew out
8 Washington chopping down the cherry tree, e.g.
9 Early 10th-century year
10 Went wild
11 Jim Carrey title role
12 Emoticon element, for short
13 Duel tool
18 NASA scrub
19 Batty
24 Like the Tin Man, upon discovery
26 Ocho ___, Jamaica
27 Conceal, as a coin
28 Where John Glenn was senator
29 "Gimme a break"
30 A Tolkien Dark Lord
34 Politico Bayh
35 Go ballistic
37 Trait carrier
39 Spa treatment
42 Baseball's Jose Canseco, by birth
44 "Me?" response
45 Ex-slave
47 First-floor apartment
48 Actor Epps
49 Davis of "The Matrix Reloaded"
50 "___ luck!"
54 Newbie
56 Realtor's goal
57 Part of A.M.
58 Chancel cross
60 Some A.L.'ers
61 West. alliance

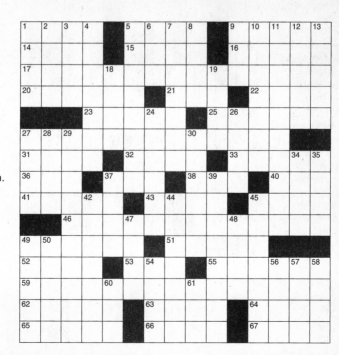

by David Sullivan

8

ACROSS
1 Baby deliverers, for short
4 Bowie's last stand
9 Sledding sites
14 Grp. bargaining with G.M.
15 Well-known
16 Barely ahead
17 *Absolutely
19 1990's treaty acronym
20 Hurler
21 Lean-to, e.g.
23 E-mail, say
24 Newspaper with hardly the highest journalistic standards
26 Olive ___
27 Psychic's field, in brief
29 Antiseptic brand
31 Backwoods refusal
34 Lock sites
37 Muck
38 Thurman of film
39 Record for later
41 Convention pin-on
43 Use a sight
44 Sorts
46 Froggy-throated
47 For instance
48 Dr. Watson portrayer Bruce
50 Decryption org.
51 "Yadda, yadda, yadda"
52 Newsman Russert
54 Land in un lago
57 San Francisco and environs
61 Like bodybuilders' bodies
63 Song from Verdi's "Un Ballo in Maschera"
64 R? . . . or a hint to the answers of the five starred clues

66 Mar. honoree
67 Critic Roger
68 Storm center
69 Choppers, so to speak
70 Shadings
71 Road surfacing material

DOWN
1 Gives the boot to
2 Wash oneself
3 *Person with whom one will always fight
4 Three or four
5 Corset tightener
6 Ethically indifferent
7 Blanc who voiced Bugs Bunny
8 Bettors' figures
9 *Cough drop flavor

10 As a whole
11 Port side
12 Cousin of a mandolin
13 Trade punches
18 Acknowledges in passing
22 "Yay!"
25 Place to play hoops
28 *It's no baloney
30 Break a commandment
31 *Aspartame brand
32 Amo follower
33 Minimum ___
34 P. & L. preparers
35 63-Across, e.g.
36 Piece together, as film
40 Heart lines: Abbr.
42 Less complex

45 Get firm
49 Lend an ear
51 Really bother
53 Anglican topper
55 Lotte of film
56 Abacus user
57 Primo
58 Johnson of "Laugh-In"
59 "Omigod!"
60 Be a lookout for, maybe
62 Brings home
65 Nigerian native

by Stephen Manion and Victor Fleming

ACROSS

1 Network to keep an "eye" on
4 Singer's sound
9 Provide for free, informally
13 Sedan or wagon
15 Ancient Peruvians
16 W.W. II general Bradley
17 "___, crackle, pop"
18 Birthplace of 59-Across
20 59-Across, e.g.
22 Having a ghost
23 Cut, as sheep's wool
24 Drunkards
25 TV program for which 59-Across won an Emmy, 1977
32 Debussy's "La ___"
34 Bullfighter's cloth
35 Melodic subject, in music
36 Album for which 59-Across won a Grammy, 1972, with "The"
41 It's a butter alternative
42 "The Wizard of Oz" pooch
43 French word before and after "à"
44 Movie for which 59-Across won an Oscar, 1961
49 The "E" in E.R.: Abbr.
50 Spicy sauce . . . or dance
53 Milan opera house
57 Play for which 59-Across won a Tony, 1975
59 Star born on 12/11/1931

61 ___ the kill
62 Lyric poems
63 Part of the head that may be congested
64 Campbell of the "Scream" movies
65 Snoozes
66 Exams
67 Jiffy

DOWN

1 Spanish houses
2 Cluster
3 Ohio's buckeye, California's redwood, etc.
4 Big shots, for short
5 Burden
6 Freezer trayful
7 Server at a drive-in
8 Aristocrat's home
9 ___ flakes
10 Forget to mention
11 Protective spray
12 Motivate
14 TV host with a book club
19 Get rid of
21 Straight up
24 Phantom
26 Scratch
27 Reuters competitor
28 Engine additive brand
29 Map borders, usually
30 Prefix with potent
31 ___ and Means Committee
32 Tabby's cry
33 French "she"
37 Foldaway bed
38 Comedian Bill, informally
39 Giant slugger Mel
40 Antlered animal
45 Tailor's line
46 "This is not making sense to me"
47 Little loved one
48 ___ to go (eager)
51 Ward (off)
52 Pre-Columbus Mexican
53 Scientologist ___ Hubbard
54 Opera set in the age of pharaohs
55 Stair part
56 Mama ___ of the Mamas and the Papas
57 Carpenter's metal piece
58 "Bonanza" brother
60 Lt.'s inferior, in the Navy

by David J. Kahn

ACROSS

1 One way to pay
7 "Mazel ___!"
10 "___ next?"
14 Illinois River city
15 "___ tu," aria sung by Renato
16 Disabled
17 Chessboard extremities
19 Suffix with corrupt
20 Tapped out
21 Grunt: Abbr.
22 Coal, essentially
24 Adventurous hero of old
27 Goodbyes
30 Temper, informally
31 Hip-hop subgenre
34 Einstein's birthplace
37 "Them!" bugs
38 Trial lawyer's advice
39 Simple rhyme scheme
40 Arctic explorer John
41 Intruder in Mr. McGregor's garden
45 $10 to $12 an hour, e.g.
47 Sans intermission, maybe
48 Some public transportation
52 The heebie-jeebies
53 Subsidy
54 Question calling for an explanation
57 Tease
58 Continental connection . . . and a hint to 17-, 24-, 31-, 41- and 48-Across
62 6 7/8, e.g.
63 Baton Rouge sch.
64 Calif. barrio locale
65 Son of Aphrodite
66 Unexplained phenomenon
67 Take from the top

DOWN

1 Popular MP3 player
2 Prefix with -itis
3 Perfume name
4 "You ___ here" (map notation)
5 Title for Isaac Newton
6 One pulling strings?
7 Extra inning
8 TV planet
9 Innards
10 Fan sounds
11 Words to a good-looker
12 DuPont fiber
13 Blockage reliever
18 G.P.A. part: Abbr.
23 "What ___!" ("That's robbery!")
24 They're tapped
25 Sweater letters
26 Pull: Fr.
27 Food thickener
28 Delany of "China Beach"
29 Between-acts musical fare
32 Perfume name
33 Feel regret for
35 Of the flock
36 Drudge on the Internet
39 Genesis victim
41 One of 12 popes
42 English-born centenarian actress Winwood
43 Track foundation
44 Singer DiFranco
46 Blows away
48 A mummy may have one
49 Studio sign
50 Accumulated
51 Purge
54 Part of a home entertainment system
55 Leer at
56 Sport
59 Long-eared beast
60 1990's Indian P.M.
61 Prefix with bar

by Levi Denham

ACROSS

1 Soprano Lehmann
6 The year 1003
10 Puzzle with a start and an end
14 Teamsters, e.g.
15 Machu Picchu builder
16 "I had no ___!"
17 *Where the Washington Nationals play
19 Salty drop
20 Before, to bards
21 Skip past
22 Orders with schmears
24 Approach at a clip
26 Not so genial
28 Pestle's partner
30 "Ho ho ho" fellow
34 Notebook projections
37 ___ Stanley Gardner
38 Intense dislike
39 When lunch might end
41 Table scrap
42 Sign of life
43 Forearm bones
44 Carnivore's intake
46 Shows curiosity
47 Many a contract negotiator
48 Prove successful
50 Montezuma, e.g.
52 Lung: Prefix
56 Basketry fiber
59 Slave away
61 Pants part
62 Folkie Guthrie
63 *Hospital diagnostic device
66 Recipe instruction
67 Milne bear
68 Cut out
69 Publicist's job
70 Sigmund Freud's daughter
71 Lets up

DOWN

1 Drew in
2 Prefix with structure
3 Takes a shine to
4 ___ Gatos, Calif.
5 Completely
6 Longish dress
7 Off-the-cuff response . . . and a hint to the answers to the four starred clues
8 Place for an R.N.
9 Metric feet
10 *Engineer from Cambridge
11 "Zip-___-Doo-Dah"
12 Gung-ho feeling
13 Floppy parts of a dachshund
18 Dean Martin's "That's ___"
23 Old Greek storyteller
25 *Gilbert and Sullivan classic
27 King Minos, for one
29 ___ l'oeil
31 Guitarist Lofgren
32 Ivory source
33 Iowa State's town
34 When said three times, a W.W. II film
35 Word jumble: Abbr.
36 Eliot's "Adam ___"
40 Gaynor of "South Pacific"
45 Something to debate
49 Loosen, as a corset
51 Buccaneers' home
53 Neighbors of 43-Across
54 Ed of the Reagan cabinet
55 Cruel sorts
56 Calamine lotion target
57 Too stylish, maybe
58 Page (through)
60 Fed. workplace watchdog
64 Director Howard
65 PBS funder

by Kenneth J. Berniker

ACROSS

1 Variety of poker
5 Actress Rowlands
9 Vice president Spiro
14 Prefix with glycemic
15 Patron saint of Norway
16 Dog's restraint
17 Unlock
18 Not all
19 "Heavens to ___!"
20 "Sahara" co-star, 2005
23 Capital of New Mexico
24 Lagasse of the Food Network
28 Shack
29 Up to, briefly
31 Prefix with tiller
32 Luggage attachment
35 Theme
37 Ukraine, e.g., once: Abbr.
38 Trip to Tahiti, for example
41 What andirons support
42 Blocked from sunlight
43 Result of a hit by a leadoff batter
44 Med. school subject
46 "Pick a card, ___ card"
47 Getting on in years
48 Shooting star
50 Italian city on the Adriatic
54 Groups collecting litter
57 Ones attracted to flames
60 ___ Hashanah
61 Landed (on)
62 Sharpshooter Oakley
63 "Puppy Love" singer Paul
64 Heredity unit
65 All gone, as food
66 Ship's petty officer, informally
67 To be: Lat.

DOWN

1 Mall units
2 Aggressive, as a personality
3 Ivy League school in Phila.
4 Words after "been there"
5 Become lenient (on)
6 Act on a sudden itching for a hitching
7 Title
8 With: Fr.
9 Photo book
10 Codger
11 Singer ___ King Cole
12 Letter before tee
13 Philosopher's question
21 Guffaws
22 Archaeological find
25 O'Donnell of "The View"
26 "___ easy to fall in love" (1977 lyric)
27 Sophia of "Two Women"
29 Fawner
30 ___-bitsy
32 Muhammad's religion
33 "Lorna ___"
34 Gently pull on
35 Average
36 Merry play
39 Stock unit
40 20 or less, at a bar
45 Computer whiz
47 Parentless child
49 With 52-Down, showbiz's Mary-Kate and Ashley
50 Walrus features
51 Tennis's Monica
52 See 49-Down
53 Cosmetician Lauder
55 Syrian or Yemeni
56 Taboo
57 Sex kitten West
58 Go ___ rampage
59 Explosive letters

by Richard Chisholm

ACROSS

1 Prince before being kissed, in a fairy tale
5 Wooden-soled shoe
10 Suddenly asks
14 Terza ___ (Italian verse form)
15 Meeting place
16 Russian city on the Oka
17 ___ about (near)
18 General Mills brand
19 Flag
20 Eating Halloween-style?
23 Cameo gem
24 Kicks
25 Bovine advertising icon
29 Russian river
31 Halloween lunch fare?
35 Name
38 "Git out!"
39 Composer David famous for "Home on the Range"
40 Spanish "but"
41 Sun or moon
42 Halloween dinner fare?
44 Andean country
45 Arctic
46 Baltimore's ___ Museum
49 ___ were
52 Healthy Halloween dish?
58 Pro ___
59 Foreword
60 Kind of trip
62 Seine summers
63 Tangle
64 Bond foe
65 Arid
66 Vehicles carrying goods to market
67 Ruin

DOWN

1 To's partner
2 Symbol of constancy
3 Melville novel
4 Clothing
5 Audited, with "on"
6 Suffering
7 Wrinkle remover
8 Algerian port
9 Story
10 Large amount of stew
11 Stellar hunter
12 Candidate of 1992 and 1996
13 Flexible Flyers
21 Big name in movie theaters
22 Resorts
25 Cities Service competitor
26 Bert who sang "If I Were King of the Forest"
27 Social-climbing type
28 Altar avowal
29 "Whoops!"
30 Clinton's attorney general
32 Frankenstein's assistant, in film
33 Ballet wear
34 Smoke
35 Hand out
36 Constellation animal
37 Physicist Niels
40 Mideast grp.
42 Cad
43 ___ no good
44 "Pretty ___"
46 1990's Israeli P.M.
47 More than tickle
48 Ad photo caption
49 Showy flower
50 Diagonal spar
51 Dungeon sight
53 Money-related: Abbr.
54 Singer Paul
55 Pakistani language
56 Of two minds
57 Grit
61 ___-wop

by Nathaniel Weiss

14

ACROSS

1 "Hold on there!"
5 Tiled art
11 Suffix with glob
14 Help for the stumped
15 Not rejecting out of hand
16 Stetson, for one
17 Particular
18 Nonsense
20 Fun time, slangily
21 Does superbly, as a stand-up comic
22 The March King
23 1988 Olympics site
25 L'Oreal competitor
26 Nonsense
30 ___ left field
31 Cast-of-thousands films
32 It may be 20%
35 Iowa State city
36 Zoo behemoth
37 Dairy Queen order
38 It begins in Mar.
39 Handed out
40 Knight stick?
41 Nonsense
43 Book boo-boos
46 Latish bedtime
47 Ready to fall out, as pages from a book
48 60's "V" sign
51 Relax, with "out"
53 Nonsense
55 Chess player's cry
56 Conditions
57 Crater Lake's state
58 Composer ___ Carlo Menotti
59 Bottom line
60 "Maybe later"
61 1070, in old Rome

DOWN

1 Taylor or Tyler, politically
2 Go 0-for-20, say
3 Bicycle or kayak, usually
4 20's dispenser
5 Alexander Calder creation
6 October birthstone
7 Broker's advice, at times
8 Added stipulations
9 Suffix in many ore names
10 Waist constrictors
11 Self-mover's rental
12 The end of one's rope?
13 Hawke of film
19 Hawk's opposite
21 Former baseball commissioner Bowie ___
24 Elevator pioneer
25 Puerto ___
26 Burlesque show props
27 Program for sobering up
28 Diner accident
29 Kunta ___ ("Roots" role)
32 In vain
33 Paycheck deduction
34 Have a look-see
36 C & W's McEntire
37 Lion tamer's workplace
39 Spoiled rotten, maybe
40 "Fatal Attraction" director Adrian
41 [I'm shocked!]
42 Museum guide
43 Like Santa's helpers
44 Pocahontas's husband
45 Cut of beef
48 Limerick writer, say
49 Fidgeting
50 Natural emollient
52 Boomers' kids
54 "___ y plata" (Montana's motto)
55 "The Wizard of Oz" studio

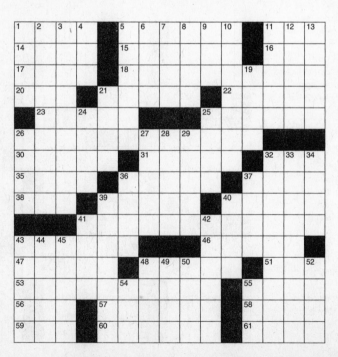

by Brendan Emmett Quigley

ACROSS

1 "So long!"
5 Burden
9 Museo in Madrid
14 Death notice
15 It follows song or slug
16 Pine exudation
17 Gets together in person
20 "Blondie" or "Beetle Bailey"
21 Tennis champ Steffi
22 Vegetable that rolls
23 Narrow street
26 Jannings of old movies
28 Confronts, with "with"
34 "___ Baba and the 40 Thieves"
35 "Kiss me" miss
36 Tangle
37 Dietary no-no for Mrs. Sprat
39 Holds on to
42 Tiny weight
43 Former Argentine dictator
45 Actress Patricia of "The Subject Was Roses"
47 Drunkard's woe, for short
48 Returns a gaze
52 Ugandan tyrant Idi ___
53 Rules, shortly
54 Pres. Lincoln
57 Urges (on)
59 "Gesundheit!" preceder
63 Strolls, as with a sweetheart
67 1950's candidate Stevenson
68 B or B+, say
69 Nobelist Wiesel

70 Irish poet who wrote "The Lake Isle of Innisfree"
71 Lambs' mothers
72 Soaks

DOWN

1 Big gobblers
2 Aid and ___
3 Layer
4 Famous Hun
5 Not at work
6 Teachers' org.
7 Grp. that patrols shores
8 Sound system
9 Opposite of losses
10 Ump
11 "Quickly!"
12 Backgammon equipment
13 Prime draft status
18 Not spare the rod

19 Domesticate
24 Bismarck's state: Abbr.
25 Toward sunrise, in Mexico
27 Yearn (for)
28 Precipitation at about 32°
29 Crown
30 Itsy-bitsy
31 Late
32 Speak from a soapbox
33 Stately shade trees
34 Austrian peaks
38 Comic Dunn formerly of "S.N.L."
40 Person of equal rank
41 Fill up
44 Unbeatable foe
46 Boston airport
49 ['Tis a pity!]

50 Capture, as one's attention
51 Shun
54 Not home
55 Requested
56 Fitzgerald, the First Lady of Jazz
58 Precipitation below 32°
60 Robust
61 "Don't bet ___!"
62 Lyric verses
64 Krazy ___
65 Mother deer
66 They're checked at checkpoints, in brief

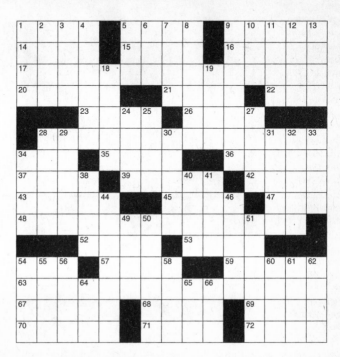

by Kurt Mengel and Jan-Michele Gianette

16

ACROSS
1 Itch site
6 Athos, Porthos and Aramis
10 With 69-Across, caped crusader player of 1966
14 Spinners' output
15 Like water under the bridge
16 Palm starch
17 Koran focus
18 Sight from a fjord
19 ___ Hubbard
20 Caped crusader player of 1989
23 Fed. watchdog
24 Fabric rib
25 Excellent
28 Bitter end?
30 Fizz producer
32 Spanish carnival
33 Butler of fiction
35 Order
37 Elbow-bender
38 Caped crusader player of 1995
41 Space station name
44 Kite part
45 Nancy of "Access Hollywood"
48 Show flexibility
50 Part of A.C.L.U.: Abbr.
52 Catty call
54 1:51, 2:51 or 3:51, e.g.
56 Put-on
58 Bruin who wore a 4
59 Caped crusader player of 1997
62 Rude response
64 Old times
65 Of service
66 Razor name
67 School for Prince William
68 Pitches
69 See 10-Across

70 Sunset shade
71 "Now you ___, now . . ."

DOWN
1 Flower part
2 Item with adjustable legs
3 Not involving check or credit
4 Wife of Jacob
5 "Ridiculous!"
6 God who killed the dragon Python at Delphi
7 27- and 41-Down, and others
8 Molokai, for one
9 Greek porticos
10 Slanting
11 Hole fixers
12 Give it ___

13 Fall football night: Abbr.
21 It's between Long Bch. and Pasadena
22 Sporting plumage
26 "Flying Down to ___"
27 With 41-Down, this puzzle's theme
29 A few: Abbr.
31 Feel low
34 Needle work?
36 Not worried about right and wrong
39 Sportage maker
40 "Shiny Happy People" band, 1991
41 See 27-Down
42 Despot Amin

43 Park sightings
46 Strong and proud
47 Rhine temptress
49 Intently view
51 Epoch of the Tertiary period
53 Most bitterly amusing
55 Doughnut shop fixture
57 Deletions
60 Head for
61 Native Nebraskan
62 Talking point?
63 Three months abroad

by Elizabeth C. Gorski

ACROSS
1 Fall (over)
5 Stadium walkways
10 At a distance
14 Wall Street letters
15 10 out of 10, e.g.
16 Western tie
17 Gambling actor?
19 Savvy about
20 Most miniature
21 Waiting room sound, maybe
22 Aloof
23 Keep ___ (persist)
25 Queue before Q
28 Gambling baseballer?
34 Pile up
36 Hydrox alternative
37 Avoiding the draft?
38 "___ Ha'i"
39 Hardhearted
40 Mrs. Dithers, in "Blondie"
41 Getting ___ years
42 Have dog breath?
43 Jerry or Jerry Lee
44 Gambling singer?
47 Take-home
48 "Queen for ___" (old TV show)
49 "Go ahead, shoot!"
51 Muscat, for one
54 Tallinn native
59 Anise-flavored liqueur
60 Gambling senator?
62 Stink
63 Hearing-related
64 Teetotalers' org.
65 Campbell of "Party of Five"
66 Feel blindly
67 Cold-shoulder

DOWN
1 Shoelace problem
2 Brontë heroine
3 In ___ (actually)
4 Téa of film
5 Steakhouse offering
6 Sidewalk stand beverages
7 5-Down, e.g.
8 Follow with a camera
9 ___-mo
10 180° turn
11 Henry Winkler role, with "the"
12 Sask. neighbor
13 Piece next to a knight
18 Barbershop boo-boos
21 1,002, in old Rome
23 Some of them are secret
24 "Iliad" locale
25 Fat cat
26 Muscat native
27 Michael of "Monty Python"
29 ___ public
30 Maine college town
31 Taken wing
32 Bone-chilling
33 You'll get a rise out of it
35 Asian city-state
39 Humane grp.
43 Popular disinfectant
45 Work of praise
46 Fight it out
50 Has memorized
51 "Tell me more"
52 Like some awakenings
53 Sea of ___ (Black Sea arm)
54 Eliel's architect son
55 Quick pic
56 Cast wearer's problem
57 Westernmost Aleutian
58 It may be proper
60 What "it" plays
61 Capek play

by Adam Cohen

18

ACROSS

1 How ham may be served in a sandwich
6 Popular kitchen wrap
11 Tiny bit, as of hair cream
14 Oscar Mayer product
15 Skip to the altar
16 Bill Joel's "___ to Extremes"
17 The Bard
19 Judges administer it
20 Hammed it up
21 Thick urban air condition
23 City where "Ulysses" is set
26 Item carried by a dog walker
28 Columbus sch.
29 "Mona Lisa" features that "follow" the viewer
32 Years, to Cicero
33 Large bays
35 PIN points
37 Concept
40 Shopping ___
41 Theme of this puzzle
42 Shopping ___
43 ___ Romeo (Italian car)
44 G.M. car
45 Birth-related
46 Ancient South American
48 Meditative exercises
50 Spanish "that"
51 Lions and tigers and bears
54 Stage comments to the audience
56 Alternative
57 Safes
60 Turncoat
61 Very scary
66 Spanish cheer
67 Synthetic fiber
68 Continental money
69 Neither's partner
70 Mexican money
71 Gaucho's rope

DOWN

1 Delivery room docs, for short
2 "I don't think so"
3 Major TV brand
4 Bumpkin
5 Foes
6 Equinox mo.
7 Out of the wind, at sea
8 All of them lead to Rome, they say
9 Tax mo.
10 Liam of "Schindler's List"
11 Rundown
12 Staring
13 Shady garden spot
18 Major TV brand
22 One of the friends on "Friends"
23 Bedrock belief
24 Commonplace
25 Waver of a red cape
27 Throw, as dice
30 Count's counterpart
31 Pore over
34 Projecting rim on a pipe
36 Japanese soup
38 Wipe out
39 World book
41 Pillow filler
45 Not as nice
47 Drive-in restaurant server
49 Grand party
51 Element with the symbol B
52 Author Calvino
53 Lesser of two ___
55 It's debatable
58 Suffix with buck
59 Big coffee holders
62 & 64 Reply to "Am too!"
63 Tax adviser's recommendation, for short
65 Fed. property overseer

by Steve Kahn

ACROSS

1 Tackle's protection
5 Indian silk center
10 Letters for a religious scholar
13 Outlet output: Abbr.
14 Funny cars might burn it
15 Curb, with "in"
17 Sports car, familiarly
18 More blue?
19 "Argghh!"
20 What fall traditionally brings
23 Intoxicating
24 Restaurant posting
25 Part of a school's Web site name
26 Shore soarer
27 "Sprechen ___ Deutsch?"
30 Annie or Dondi, of the comics
32 Collectors' goals
34 Hydrocarbon suffixes
37 Staff members: Abbr.
38 Ones responding to 20-Across
41 "Git!"
44 Mess overseers: Abbr.
45 Bounders
49 Easy marks
51 Old White House inits.
53 "Nope"
54 Suffix with human
55 Luxury
58 Screwball
60 What 38-Across might take
64 Sportswear brand
65 Shot from a tee
66 Word before and after "à"
67 Back-to-school mo.

68 Like some shoes and drinks
69 Actresses Balin and Claire
70 1965 Ursula Andress film
71 ___ nous
72 Cig. boxes

DOWN

1 Beauties
2 "None missing"
3 Not giving in one bit
4 Throw hot water on
5 Pro's foe
6 "Your majesty"
7 Drang's counterpart
8 Am I, doubled
9 Rita of "West Side Story"

10 Track race
11 Sly laughs
12 Patronized, as a restaurant
16 One result of a perfect game
21 Fleur-de-___
22 Presences
28 It makes "adverb" an adjective
29 Cuts off
31 Infinitesimal division of a min.
33 Did laps, say
35 Grade A item
36 Clockmaker Thomas
39 Louvre pyramid architect
40 Tilde's shape, loosely
41 Pooh-poohs
42 Spicy ingredients

43 Leader in a holiday song
46 As old as the hills
47 Upper Midwesterner
48 Social problem
50 Sit on it
52 Pan Am competitor
56 S. C. Johnson wrap
57 Boot
59 Cobwebby area
61 Monitor's measure
62 Assert
63 Turn over

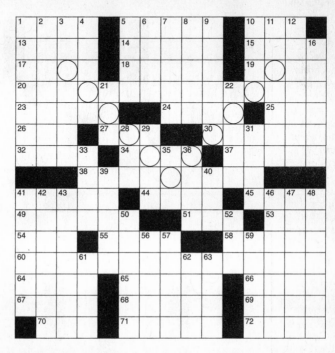

by Patrick Merrell

ACROSS

1 Asian nannies
6 Ending with land or sea
11 Legal org.
14 Josh ___, who directed and co-produced "South Pacific"
15 Inventor Howe
16 Right this minute
17 Skylit areas
18 Pipsqueaks
19 Genetic material
20 Items on some necklaces
22 Actor Estrada
23 Colorful tropical fish
24 Lacking vigor
26 Swing on an axis
29 Minor railroad stop
32 The first or fifth letter of George
34 DeMille films
35 Overly
36 Simulate, as an old battle
39 "Where ___?"
42 Goethe classic
43 Early evening hour
45 1998 Sandra Bullock film
50 Bronx Bomber
51 Comfortable with
52 Life of Riley
54 Parts of bridles
55 Words that can precede the starts of 20-, 29- and 45- Across
61 Grand ___ (wine words)
62 Mob scenes
63 Column style
64 Feel sick
65 Gas in a layer
66 Flash of light
67 Free TV spot: Abbr.
68 Obsolete VCR's
69 Brief brawl

DOWN

1 [sigh]
2 Closet invader
3 Taj Mahal site
4 Cafeteria headwear
5 Adder, e.g.
6 Williams of tennis
7 Hint
8 "___ it the truth!"
9 Pitiful
10 Tricky curve
11 Dissident Sakharov
12 Mackerellike fish
13 Rise and shine
21 Wrecker's job
22 Young newts
25 What Sgt. Friday sought
26 It's not breaking the sound barrier anymore
27 London facility
28 ET's ride
30 Busybody
31 Place for sweaters?
33 Transplant, of a sort
37 Praise posthumously
38 "___ Beso" (1962 hit)
39 Gardner of Hollywood
40 Stag attendees
41 Sign, as a deal
42 A.T.F. agents, e.g.
44 Mask opening
45 Lug nuts' cover
46 Husband of Isis
47 "Downtown" singer Clark
48 Acts the coquette
49 Used a bench
53 Drinks from a flask
56 Radish or carrot
57 European erupter
58 "What's ___ for me?"
59 Salon job
60 Prefix with plasm
62 Stick up

by Nancy Kavanaugh

ACROSS
1 The "D" of D.J.
5 Huge hit
10 Nile reptiles
14 Great Salt Lake's state
15 Cosmetician Lauder
16 Junk e-mail
17 "The Price Is Right" phrase
19 Trig function
20 Eugene O'Neill's "___ for the Misbegotten"
21 Some necklines do this
23 Flatters, with "up"
26 Egypt's capital
27 2004 Olympics city
28 Made a cashless transaction
31 Accomplisher
32 Up, on a map
33 Chicago-to-Atlanta dir.
34 Factory-emissions testing grp.
35 "The Weakest Link" phrase
37 Photo ___ (picture-taking times)
38 Cotton ___
39 Bassoon's smaller cousins
40 Et ___ (and others)
41 Protective wear for airborne toxins
43 Wonder to behold
45 Nursery supplies
46 "___ Gump"
47 Oreo fillings
49 Wonderland cake message
50 Loooong sandwich
51 "Family Feud" phrase

56 Wading bird
57 Painting stand
58 Cafeteria carrier
59 Space shuttle launcher
60 Attire
61 "The ___ the limit"

DOWN
1 French nobleman
2 "How was ___ know?"
3 ___ Adams, patriot with a beer named after him
4 One peeking at answers on a test
5 Spanish gents
6 1980's PC's ran on it
7 Lots and lots
8 Finish, with "up"
9 All-female get-together
10 State confidently to
11 "Wheel of Fortune" phrase
12 Sign of hunger
13 "Peter Pan" pirate
18 Future indicator
22 Like a ballerina's body
23 No-goodnik
24 Paradise
25 "Jeopardy!" phrase
26 Atkins diet concerns, briefly
28 ___ well (is a good sign)
29 Glimpses
30 Make potable, as sea water

32 Partner of crannies
35 Flip out
36 Fanatical
40 Handcuffs
42 Brunch cocktail
43 Roadside stops
44 The Cadets, in college sports
46 Ones you just adore
47 Goatee's locale
48 Singer McEntire
49 Gaelic tongue
52 Former Mideast grp.
53 Noah's craft
54 Palindromic cheer
55 Part of CBS: Abbr.

by Jim Hyres

22

ACROSS

1 Rockette launchers?
5 Combo's cue
10 Stereo knob
14 Like crazy
15 Cordial flavoring
16 With the bow, in music
17 "Kiss Me Kate" co-star, 1953
19 Time for a revolution
20 One of the Fab Four
21 State nicknamed "Small Wonder"
23 Mideast flash point
26 "The __ Daba Honeymoon"
27 The Red Baron, e.g.
30 "Diner" actor
36 Press for payment
37 What well-thrown 44-Across do
38 This is one
39 Parasite supporter
41 Cambridge univ.
42 Seek food, perhaps
43 Sequel novel to "Typee"
44 Hail Marys, e.g.
47 Part of D.J.I.A.
48 1945 Peace Nobelist
50 Med. specialty
51 Certain investment, for short
52 "La Vie en Rose" singer
54 Chinese potable
59 Driving hazard
63 Sit around
64 Utah senator
67 The Pointer Sisters' "__ Excited"
68 Pointed arch
69 Cut back
70 "Cold one"
71 Having bumps
72 Leave slack-jawed

DOWN

1 Lionized actor?
2 H. G. Wells race
3 Cap's partner
4 College football's Grand Old Man
5 Taken
6 Press, slangily
7 50–50, say
8 What a nod might mean
9 Spill one's guts
10 Show set in Hawaii
11 Atlas stat
12 Mark for life
13 Like some losers
18 Arteries
22 Six-pack __
24 Sound on "Batman"
25 Brutish sort
27 Not permanent
28 Former New York governor
29 David of CNN
31 Dander
32 Really enjoys
33 Shake off
34 Yak, yak, yak . . .
35 Packaging abbr.
40 Super-delicious
44 1986 Best Picture
45 Quarterback Manning
46 More than trim
49 East ender?
53 Tries to fly
54 Like a slickster
55 Spanish Steps city
56 Facility
57 "Sum" preceder
58 Far from arable
60 Louis XIV, self-referentially
61 Linen hue
62 Not now
65 Stick-to-it-__
66 Sparks on the screen

by Adam Cohen

ACROSS
1 Spills the beans
6 Got along
11 Epitome of simplicity
14 Accountants may run one
15 Entanglement
17 Said with a sneer
18 Garb for Tarzan
19 Eskimo building material
20 Bill of Rights defender, in brief
22 ___ voce (quietly)
23 "Maybellene" singer
27 Cries like a wolf
28 ___ Constitution
29 Three-legged piece
31 Stir up
34 Certain seat request
36 Suffix with fictional
39 Grimm brothers fairy tale
43 Popular fuel additive
44 Reveal
45 Openly mourned
46 Send (to)
48 Menu phrase
50 Lots and lots
52 Indirect
58 Inamoratas
60 Horn sound
61 Bearded animal
62 The starts of 18-, 23-, 39- and 52-Across
65 Spiral
67 Crystal-clear
68 Rugged ridge
69 Every other hurricane
70 Like music
71 Stallions' interests

DOWN
1 Underlying
2 Something for friends to "do"
3 A fond farewell
4 Wish
5 Butchers' offerings
6 Girl: Fr.
7 ___ propre
8 Baseball stat.
9 Sea eagle
10 Diagnosers
11 Similar
12 Itty-___
13 Some salmon
16 Boston newspaper
21 "CSI" network
24 Cosby's "I Spy" co-star
25 Amber or copal
26 Everyone, in the South
30 Toy train purchase
31 Trains: Abbr.
32 Passé
33 Not follow the book
34 Houston pro
35 "What was ___ think?"
37 Rush (along)
38 Tolkien creature
40 Jolly old ___ (Santa)
41 Lothario's look
42 Gun barrel cleaner
47 Other side
48 Big fuss
49 Philadelphia landmark hotel
50 French peaks
51 Religious parchment
53 Unadulterated
54 Pried (into)
55 Eyeballer
56 Conglomerate
57 Frequent Astaire wear
59 Genesis brother
63 Sebastian who once ran the world's fastest mile
64 Dos Passos work
66 Century 21 competitor

by James R. Leeds

24

ACROSS
1 Used a broom
6 Opened just a crack
10 Doesn't guzzle
14 Place for a barbecue
15 "Uh-uh"
16 Threaded fastener
17 Proverb
18 Managed, with "out"
19 ___ avis (unusual one)
20 Bathroom fixture sales representative?
23 Way to the top of a mountain?
26 Stave off
27 Hanging sculpture in Alabama?
32 Alleviated
33 Words said on the way out the door
34 E.M.T.'s skill
37 Pub drinks
38 Gasps for air
39 "Scram!"
40 Dashed
41 Sunday newspaper color feature
42 Continue downhill without pedaling
43 Warsaw refinement?
45 G-rated
48 Accustoms
49 Majestic summer time?
54 Solar emissions
55 Really big show
56 Lubricated
60 Victim of a prank
61 Choir voice
62 State fund-raiser
63 Retired fliers, for short

64 Spinks or Trotsky
65 Company in a 2001–02 scandal

DOWN
1 Hot springs locale
2 Bankroll
3 When a plane should get in: Abbr.
4 Dirty places
5 Initial progress on a tough problem
6 From a fresh angle
7 Wisecrack
8 Copycat
9 Cincinnati team
10 Endeavored
11 Dumbstruck
12 Less adulterated
13 Sudden jump

21 Be behind in payments
22 50/50 share
23 Besmirch
24 Down Under critter
25 "A Doll's House" playwright
28 Dolphins' venue
29 Onetime Dodges
30 Mess up
31 Contingencies
34 Committee head
35 Search party
36 Some I.R.A.'s, informally
38 One in the legislative biz
39 "Eureka!" cause
41 Swindles
42 TV cabinet
43 Purposes of commas

44 Little, in Lille
45 Deck of 52
46 Hawaiian feasts
47 "Aïda" setting
50 Bluish green
51 Car rod
52 "What've you been ___?"
53 Hired thug
57 Epistle: Abbr.
58 W.W. II arena
59 Underworld boss

by Seth A. Abel

ACROSS

1 Blue-ribbon position
6 Tiny aquatic plant
10 Radar screen dot
14 Thespian
15 "Crazy" bird
16 Moreno of "West Side Story"
17 School essay
18 Pepper's partner
19 "Oh, woe!"
20 Start of a comment by critic George Jean Nathan
23 Like hen's teeth
26 "I surrender!"
27 Part 2 of the comment
32 Washington Mayor Marion
33 Sharpens
34 Puppy's bite
37 Opera singer Pinza
38 Virile
39 Zola courtesan
40 Kind of whisky
41 Ill-fated ship Andrea ___
42 Olympian's prize
43 Part 3 of the comment
45 Atlantic fish
48 Fish-eating hawk
49 End of the comment
54 Helps
55 Natural balm
56 Prefix with -pedic
60 Prefix with logical
61 Not the front or back
62 Arctic, for one
63 Sign gas
64 "___ Dreams" (1994 documentary film)
65 Nairobi's land

DOWN

1 More than hefty
2 "___ bin ein Berliner"
3 Expy., e.g.
4 Hat for a siesta
5 Excessively sweet
6 As well
7 Goof off
8 Game on a green
9 Not pro
10 Intellectually gifted
11 State flower of New Hampshire
12 "Darn ___!"
13 Old hat
21 Joey ___ & the Starliters (60's group)
22 Chicago team
23 Cavalry sword
24 Nutso
25 Eagle's nest
28 Swiss ___ (vegetable)
29 Gin's partner
30 China's Zhou ___
31 Actress Susan
34 Ralph who wrote "Unsafe at Any Speed"
35 Silly
36 Very friendly
38 Dairy farm sound
39 Chief Joseph's tribe
41 Dumbbell
42 Identified wrongly
43 Special boy
44 Overly
45 Beau
46 Rebuke
47 Bucking bronco event
50 "Candy / Is dandy . . ." humorist
51 Mishmash
52 Kind of list
53 Mondale or Quayle, e.g.
57 Countdown start
58 Cow chow
59 Go ___ diet

by Pauline V. Wilson

ACROSS

1 Sixth sense
4 Sprightly dances
8 Egypt's Sadat
13 Designer Cassini
15 Taj Mahal site
16 Bellini opera
17 Caretaker for a baby
18 Sticky stuff
19 Gnawed
20 Austrian observance of April 30
23 Meadow
24 Like wind chimes
25 British observance of April 23
31 Onetime Argentine leader
32 ___ Perot
33 How to address a Fr. lady
36 The Emerald Isle
37 Airport abbr.
38 Ukraine's capital
39 Prevail
40 Fisher's rental
42 Stretched tight
43 Indian observance of April 13
45 Connecting strips of land
48 Trivial Pursuit need
49 United States observance of April 14
55 Perform penance
56 Evictee from paradise
57 ___ Bator
59 Deluxe sheet material
60 One-liner, e.g.
61 Aggregate
62 Golf great Sam
63 Stout relatives
64 Mack or Danson

DOWN

1 Ages and ages
2 Order at KFC
3 Pitcher Alejandro
4 Black-spotted cat
5 Composer Stravinsky
6 Seaman's quaff
7 H. H. Munro's pseudonym
8 Biblical liar
9 Zilch
10 Jalopy
11 Menotti hero
12 Worn-out
14 Old fighting vessel
21 Lowly worker
22 Rules: Abbr.
25 Gush forth
26 Hatcher of "Lois & Clark"
27 Happy face
28 Accra's land
29 Bobble
30 Newswoman Tabitha
33 Warship danger
34 Tableland
35 At any time
38 Excited
40 Praise
41 "I cannot tell ___"
42 Double
43 Grammy-winning Twain
44 "My Cup Runneth Over" singer, 1967
45 Bridge declaration
46 Beelzebub
47 Savings vehicle, briefly
50 Punjabi prince
51 Screen fave
52 Bake sale order
53 Came to rest
54 New Haven school
58 Composer Rorem

by D. J. DeChristopher

ACROSS

1 Inside the foul line
5 Like Ionesco's soprano
9 Romantic actor Charles
14 It parallels the radius
15 Perlman of "Pearl"
16 A month in Madrid
17 Robin
19 Actress Shire
20 Wall Street order
21 Brain test results, for short
23 Some linemen: Abbr.
24 Hopes
28 School failure
30 Alphabetic run
31 Kind of summit
33 All over
34 Pinkish color
36 Custard tart
38 Longtime Israeli foreign minister
41 Rock concert equipment
42 See 32-Down
43 Start of a Latin boast
44 ___ Alto, Calif.
45 Mobil rival
46 E-mail predecessor
47 Oklahoma city
49 1995 earthquake site
51 Potash
52 Conniver
55 Having deep pockets
57 Miler Sebastian
58 French tire
60 Shot over the head
61 D-Day beach
63 Legal-tender bill

68 Situation for Pauline?
69 Ice cream thickener
70 Industrial show
71 First name in cosmetics
72 Mother of Apollo
73 ___ ex machina

DOWN

1 Raccoon, e.g.
2 Bitter
3 Not the party type: Abbr.
4 Browning's Ben Ezra, e.g.
5 Supreme Court Justice Stephen
6 "Gotcha!"
7 ___-majeste
8 Saw
9 Trusts

10 ___ roll
11 Chicken, so to speak
12 "A Masked Ball" aria
13 Friars Club event
18 Part of R.F.D.
22 Super-duper
24 Royalties org.
25 Pore in a leaf
26 Service award
27 "60 Minutes" newsman
29 Irk
32 With 42-Across, a famous pirate
35 Together
37 Woolf's "___ of One's Own"
39 Words before and after "for"
40 Forbade

42 When doubled, a German city
46 Mortise's mate
48 Stick
50 Ravel composition
52 Sub's eye, for short
53 Shows up
54 Buick model
56 Fell off
59 Feel the ___
62 Make haste
64 Dinner table exhortation
65 Fire
66 Computer's heart, for short
67 Dempsey stat

by Mark Elliot Skolsky

28

ACROSS

1 Garbage boat
5 Ingrid's "Casablanca" role
9 I.O.U.'s
14 Singer Guthrie
15 "Get a ___ of that!"
16 Nouveau ___
17 Nightgown-clad nursery-rhyme character
20 Reverse image, for short
21 ___ the lily
22 Be present at
23 Grow dim
24 Jackie's second husband
25 Heavens
26 Saying of Caesar
31 Banishment
32 Put on
33 No, to Nikita
37 Towering
38 Item
40 Snapshot, Mad. Ave.-style
41 Captain Hook's assistant
42 Tic-tac-toe win
43 Nearsighted Mr.
44 1960 Terry-Thomas film farce
48 Tie the knot
51 Fleur-de-___
52 Bloody
53 Twenty questions category
55 Concerning
56 Alternative to a subway
59 Shakespearean comedy (original spelling)
62 Smooth and glossy
63 Persian sprite
64 Brainstorm
65 "___ la vista, baby!"
66 Former spouses
67 Bruce or Laura of Hollywood

DOWN

1 Cut, as a log
2 Prairie Indian
3 Designer Cassini
4 "Unbelievable!"
5 Fighting ___ (Big Ten team)
6 Lounged around
7 Port ___, Egypt
8 Summer cooler
9 Rex Reed, e.g.
10 Help for the puzzled
11 Bill Clinton's staffer Harold
12 Use your brain
13 Squalid
18 "___ at the office"
19 Bandleader Fred
23 Actor Dafoe
24 Door-to-door cosmetics company
26 Docs for dachshunds
27 Quiz
28 Cairo's river
29 Dialect
30 Odious reputation
34 Berra or Bear
35 Prince William's school
36 Grabbed
38 "___ a Mockingbird"
39 Works in the garden
43 French mothers
45 Where Nome is home
46 Pay no heed to
47 Action star Chuck
48 Former 49ers coach Bill
49 W.W. II's ___ Gay
50 Jackknife and others
54 Encounter
55 Wild goat
56 Presage
57 Exploiter
58 Getz or Kenton
60 Imitate
61 Pot top

by Stephanie Spadaccini

ACROSS

1 State firmly
5 Born's partner
9 Famous rib donor
13 Heart
14 Stead
15 Teacake
16 Like Hawthorne's "Tales"
18 Peer
19 "My Fair Lady" scene
20 Second-stringer
22 Five-to-one, e.g.
26 St. Teresa of ___
28 Some stock buys
30 Galley type appropriate for this puzzle?
32 Speaker's place
33 "Darn!"
35 Pretend
36 Addl. telephone off a main line
37 Hamlet
39 Rita Hayworth spouse ___ Khan
40 Page of music
42 Speak to the hard-of-hearing?
43 Dog biter
44 Has contempt for
46 Alternative to Nikes
48 Valued violin
49 Publish lies about
50 Queen ___ lace
52 Short trip
56 Compel
58 Extra-base hit
62 Contract signer
63 Official language of Pakistan
64 Vogue rival
65 Head honcho
66 Tournament passes
67 Fine pajama material

DOWN

1 Official proceedings
2 Wedding exchange
3 The Red
4 45's and 78's
5 Sandwich order
6 ___ Bravo
7 Slippery one
8 Garb
9 Get
10 Gobbledygook
11 Santa ___ (Pacific wind)
12 Sportscaster Allen
15 Sycophantic
17 And more
21 It'll take you for a ride
23 Spelling of "Beverly Hills 90210"
24 "Paradise of exiles": Shelley
25 Workers in stables
27 Soap plants
28 Mexican state
29 " "
31 One-named Irish singer
32 Assts.
34 Oregon's capital
37 Ernest or Julio Gallo
38 Elation
41 Hypnotic states
43 Searches for provisions
45 "Sprechen ___ Deutsch?"
47 Lower California, familiarly
51 Ticket remainder
53 Good fruit with a bad name?
54 Dickens girl
55 Quite a trip
56 Stretch the truth
57 Warbler Yoko
59 Kind of humor
60 Lyric poem
61 School transportation

by Eileen Lexau

ACROSS

1 Portend
5 Over
9 Short and maybe sweet
14 A party to
15 Where the Villa Borghese is
16 Massage
17 Movie short about a perfectly timed ape?
20 Frame
21 Sped
22 Wild party
23 Teri of "Tootsie"
25 Auto import from Europe
27 Cummerbund
30 Movie short about arrestin' writer Anita?
35 It's unsmelted
36 Early Brit
37 Deem appropriate
38 City for Miss Kitty
40 Plop or plunk starter
42 ___-mouthed
43 Brunch fare
45 Actor Calhoun
47 Set
48 Movie short about a tireless parent?
50 "One man's ___ is another man's Persian"
51 O'Casey or Penn
52 Slightly open
54 Maladies, worries, etc.
57 Withdraw by degrees
59 Levi's "Christ Stopped at ___"
63 Movie short about Capone in court?
66 Sub detector
67 Small songster
68 Astronaut Armstrong
69 Jumbo shrimp
70 ___ buco
71 Small boat

DOWN

1 Opinion of others?
2 In times past
3 Blockhead
4 "Stop already!"
5 Two-by-two craft
6 Emergency hauler
7 "Typee" sequel
8 Repeat without thinking
9 Ring result
10 Official class member
11 Kind of guard or end
12 Trilled
13 On pins and needles
18 I.R.S. employee
19 French military caps
24 Baseball stat
26 Adversary
27 Sin city
28 Free bakery "promotion"
29 Matzoh time
31 Back of a boat
32 Over 21
33 Half-seas over
34 Fashion
36 P.G.A.'s Calvin
39 Vulnerable boxer's point
41 Woos
44 Warms up
46 British rule in India
49 Boxer's combo
50 007, to Goldfinger
53 W.W. I army: Abbr.
54 Stinger
55 ___ about (approximately)
56 Author Ferber
58 Tunes
60 It's a cookie
61 Beastly home
62 In a sick way
64 Vase
65 Musician Brian

by Manny Nosowsky

ACROSS

1 One of the Three Bears
5 Dog restraint
10 "___ It Romantic?"
14 Misfortunes
15 Dramatist Edward
16 Swirl with a spoon
17 School cutup
19 Moon goddess
20 Basic belief
21 "You said it!"
22 Garden of Eden man
23 Slept noisily
25 Muscular
27 Pony's gait
29 Like some committees
32 Young 'uns
35 Between-meals eater
39 Hubbub
40 Drink cooler
41 Art student's subject
42 On, as a lamp
43 Pie ___ mode
44 Longtime PBS series
45 Artist Paul
46 Kind of sentence
48 ". . . one ___ two!" (Welk intro)
50 Gobbles (up)
54 Wreck, as a train
58 1970 Kinks hit
60 Poker players' markers
62 Catch cowboy-style
63 "We try harder" company
64 Head of P.E. class
66 ___-majeste
67 "Stand and Deliver" star Edward James ___
68 Mister, in Munich
69 Pretentiously cultured
70 Harvests
71 "That's clear"

DOWN

1 Early Brits
2 Revolutionary hero Ethan
3 City in north Texas
4 Declares
5 Fond du ___, Wis.
6 Scat queen Fitzgerald
7 Manhattan Project project
8 Underground passage
9 Redhead's dye
10 Cuba, e.g.
11 Quiet schoolroom
12 Ship of 1492
13 Coal car
18 Suffix with trick or prank
24 Fashion's Karan
26 Cautious
28 Perfectly
30 "Garfield" dog
31 Pigeon's home
32 Fibber
33 Rights defender, for short
34 Honor for the A-team?
36 Alphabet trio
37 Dance at a Jewish wedding
38 Improve
41 "The King and I" governess
45 Pakistani port
47 Playwright Sean
49 Oscar ___ Renta
51 Hardship
52 Christopher Morley's "Kitty ___"
53 Highest, in honors
55 Grave matter?
56 River to the Rhone
57 Actor Peter
58 Bit of a song refrain
59 Partner of "done with"
61 "Knock it off!"
65 Road curve

by Fran and Lou Sabin

ACROSS
1 Help in a heist
5 Neighbor of St. Pete
10 ___ podrida
14 Etna output
15 "Our Town" role
16 Close
17 Cereal "for kids"
18 Pitcher Ryan
19 Restrain
20 John Stuart Mill treatise
22 Senator Hatch
23 Airport sched. abbr.
24 "Erotica" singer
26 Part of a place setting
30 Angola's capital
32 Stinging wasp
34 Amtrak stop: Abbr.
35 Colorless
39 Party to a defense treaty
40 Old-time anesthetic
42 Cunning trick
43 Fluctuate repeatedly
44 West of Hollywood
45 Sadistic sort
47 Diamond arbiter
50 Small fry
51 Spat
54 Early Beatle Sutcliffe
56 Single entities
57 In a precarious situation
63 "Make ___" (captain's directive)
64 Astronomer Tycho
65 Just
66 Scrabble piece
67 Russo and Magritte

68 Christmas tree topper
69 Bullring cheers
70 Idolize
71 Bill Clinton's birthplace

DOWN
1 Like Charlie Parker's sax
2 Farm building
3 Wicked
4 It's hailed by city dwellers
5 Principle
6 Lacking principles
7 Jazz bassist Hinton
8 Schoolyard friend
9 Novelist Rand
10 1963 Drifters song
11 Live's partner

12 What Mr. Chips taught
13 Gladiator's place
21 Nota ___
22 Peculiar
25 Cost ___ and a leg
26 Open carriage
27 Sport shirt
28 Paris airport
29 Rodgers and Hart musical
31 Theater employee
33 Site of Super Bowl XXX
36 Milieu for Lemieux
37 "I cannot tell ___"
38 Hive dwellers
41 Fitted
46 Sundries case
48 "___ Doubtfire"
49 Book before Job

51 Capital just south of the equator
52 "Wait ___ Dark"
53 Supermarket section
55 "___ Eyes" (1969 song)
58 Prefix meaning "one-billionth"
59 Snack
60 Passionately studying
61 Thunder sound
62 Bronte heroine
64 Maidenform product

by Gregory E. Paul

ACROSS

1 Fleming and others
5 Ulan __
10 Masseur's target
14 Fail to mention
15 "Penny wise, pound foolish," e.g.
16 Word with monkey or minor
17 Plumbers' favorite film?
19 Carolina __
20 Star-shaped
21 Tiny brain size
22 "__ boy!"
23 Plumbers' favorite fishing item?
25 Winter wear
27 Teased, in a way
29 Cultivated
32 "I read you"
35 Protuberance
37 Keats piece
38 A.P. competitor
39 Devoted fans
41 Population at the time of 44-Across
42 Seance sound
43 Certain base
44 See 41-Across
45 Makes teary
47 Noblemen
50 Rorschach patterns
52 Plumbers' favorite anthropologist?
55 Kapow!
57 Patient reply, maybe
59 Looked impolitely
61 Early Tarzan player Lincoln
62 Plumbers' favorite address?
64 Linen vestments
65 Large book
66 Pigeon's home
67 Spar
68 Booby trap
69 Greek vowels

DOWN

1 "State Fair" state
2 Aggregate
3 Capone contemporary
4 Without a smile
5 Wailed
6 Bustle
7 Canvas
8 Checks out, in a way
9 Editor
10 Like an eddy
11 Plumbers' favorite baseball player?
12 Hastens
13 Sicilian spouter
18 Toothy tool
24 Helicopter part
26 Broadcasts
28 Hospital cry
30 Author Ferber
31 Judge
32 Taxi's drop-off point
33 Kind of glass
34 Plumbers' favorite weapons?
36 One may be precious
39 Bygone hairstyle
40 Spinning wheel attachments
44 Sideways
46 Nearly
48 Do a blacksmith's repair job
49 They follow so
51 Drawing room
53 Grain disease
54 Gossip
55 Smile
56 Cooking pot
58 Sinuous dance
60 Henna and indigo
63 How to address a knight

by Michael S. Maurer

ACROSS

1 Dish of leftovers
5 Ink problem
9 Ill-tempered woman
14 Turkish official
15 Money to buy a car, maybe
16 Kind of fairy
17 1981 Treat Williams film
20 Followers of Xerxes
21 Socks cover them
22 Nevertheless
23 Weep
24 Groups entering Noah's ark
25 Yield, as a dividend
26 Actress Arthur and others
27 Taxi
30 Knight's horse
33 Jai ___
34 Middling
35 1945 Mel Torme song
38 Thin
39 Start of a counting-out rhyme
40 Like an old bucket of song
41 Memorable period
42 E-mail, e.g.
43 "It's freezing!"
44 Fountain order
45 Butt
46 ___ Vegas
49 Mail-related
52 Spy for the U.S.
54 1996 Hillary Clinton best seller
56 Purloined
57 More than ajar
58 ___ of Man
59 Crossed one's fingers
60 Ice block
61 Toot

DOWN

1 One of the Seven Dwarfs
2 Go along (with)
3 Polo or tee
4 Storied boy with silver skates
5 Not sharp, as eyesight
6 Off one's rocker
7 Clods
8 Explosive
9 Ones copying from Dictaphones
10 Pawns
11 Disturb
12 Suffix with kitchen
13 Philosophers' questions
18 Loud insect
19 Michener best seller
24 Moist-eyed
25 Job benefit
26 Mixture
27 Boil or broil
28 "___ forgive our debtors"
29 Former German capital
30 Enticing store sign
31 Ivan or Nicholas
32 Sicilian mount
33 Rocket stage
34 Lead player
36 Compass part
37 Everyday
42 Wet through and through
43 Sheep noise
44 Unfresh
45 Missouri or Delaware
46 Renter's paper
47 Polygon's corner
48 At quite an incline
49 "Nonsense!"
50 Palindromic emperor
51 Halt
52 Superman attire
53 Silver-tongued
55 Weep

by Marilynn Huret

ACROSS
1 Half a school yr.
4 Part of CD
8 Brings home
13 "American Gigolo" actor
14 Capri, e.g.
15 German sub
16 Halo
17 "Coming of Age in Samoa" author
18 Tycoon J. Paul ___
19 60's singer who "walks like a man"-servant?
22 Chinese gambling game
23 Sprinted
24 "Yuck!"
27 Airport abbr.
28 Ancient Brit
31 Actress Reynolds
33 Talks up, so to speak
35 Depend (on)
36 Life-style expert who's a perfect housekeeper?
40 Bargain seeker's event
41 Radio woe
42 Sign of acne
45 Basics
46 ___ Lanka
49 Critic ___ Louise Huxtable
50 Paris's ___ de la Cite
52 Miss Prynne of "The Scarlet Letter"
54 PBS host who's good in the kitchen?
57 Nichelle Nichols's role on "Star Trek"
60 ___ Fein
61 Lariat
62 Folk or rap, e.g.
63 Awestruck
64 Ripened
65 Environs
66 Hankerings
67 Fenced-in area

DOWN
1 "Sunday in the Park With George" painter
2 Gofer's chore
3 Intended
4 Reduce in size
5 "You're clear"
6 Eastern European
7 Lebanese tree
8 Conductor Ormandy
9 Assist in crime
10 Degenerate badly
11 Revolutionist Turner
12 Pigpen
13 Faux pas
20 Fini
21 Young chap
24 Above, in Berlin
25 Decorate expensively
26 "Watch it!"
29 Cartoonist Addams
30 Head, in Italy
32 Bric-a-___
33 Get ready, for short
34 Pierce
36 One of "the help"
37 ___ mater
38 Some prints
39 Older but ___
40 Health resort
43 Walt Whitman bloomers
44 Actor Wallach
46 Moe, for one
47 Begin again, as a debate
48 Annoyed
51 Russell Baker specialty
53 Leftover piece
54 Operatic solo
55 Buster Brown's dog
56 Any day now
57 She played June in "Henry & June"
58 "Ben-___"
59 Exploit

by Stephanie Spadaccini

36

ACROSS

1 Stumble
5 1962 Best Picture setting
11 Eye
14 Layers
15 Party items
16 Partner of neither
17 The "E. B" of E. B. White
19 Literary monogram
20 Car heater setting
21 Opposed
22 Shack
23 All things considered
25 ___ fell swoop
27 The "H. G." of H. G. Wells
32 Overfill
33 Rakes
34 Sonnet measure
38 On again
41 Stomach woe
42 Relationship
44 "Mi chiamano Mimi," e.g.
46 The "A. A." of A. A. Milne
51 Chief Bolshevik
52 Having visions in one's head?
55 "I Love Rock 'n Roll" singer Joan
57 Queen's home
60 Sister of Urania
61 One called "The Lion of God"
62 The "J. D." of J. D. Salinger
64 S.A.S. competitor
65 Philly team
66 Unabridged, e.g.
67 Shoe width
68 "The Other" author and others
69 Wows

DOWN

1 Silents actress Bara
2 Get a new tenant for
3 On the good side of
4 Cupid's love
5 Andrews or Maguire, e.g.: Abbr.
6 ___ avis
7 Bard's river
8 Flub a grounder
9 Bothering
10 Ninny
11 Busy-busy
12 Wine choice
13 Raised
18 Approaches
22 Catch for a Florida fisherman
24 Skier's aid
26 Atop, poetically
28 Automne preceder
29 Chill, so to speak
30 Car since 1989
31 Sum, es, ___
34 "Make ___ good one!"
35 Be sick
36 When to ring a bell, maybe
37 Intelligence test developer
39 Money for an A.A.R.P. member
40 Louise of "Gilligan's Island"
43 A Bobbsey twin
45 Like a certain attraction
47 2-D
48 Power
49 Goofs
50 Admit again
53 Words before "to rend" and "to sew"
54 Manners
55 The Fatman's TV partner
56 Glamour rival
58 Alone
59 U.S. govt. agents
62 "West Side Story" gang member
63 Kind of curve

by Richard Hughes

ACROSS

1 Came apart at the seams
5 Ann ___, Mich.
10 Without
14 Mimics
15 Actress Rigg
16 Show appreciation at a concert
17 Complimentary close
19 ___ mater
20 Smeltery input
21 Old-fashioned poems
22 More sedate
24 Muffin ingredient
26 Shrewd
27 German spa
28 Deli side order
31 Spanish houses
34 Singer Crystal
35 Flamenco exclamation
36 Desertlike
37 Brooklyn's ___ Island
38 Czar before Feodor I
39 Ballpoint, e.g.
40 University of Florida footballer
41 ___ Litovsk (1918 treaty site)
42 Quit for the day
44 Pod occupant
45 Ice skating figure
46 With 43-Down, a complimentary close
50 Old Iran
52 ___ Lee cakes
53 Madhouse, so to speak
54 Guinness and others
55 Complimentary close
58 Madden

59 Formal goodbye
60 Kind of hygiene
61 Lock openers
62 "You've got the wrong guy!"
63 Nota ___

DOWN

1 Forbidden
2 Soap ___
3 Change, as a clock
4 Superlative suffix
5 Sneaker brand
6 Out of bed
7 "A Christmas Carol" cries
8 Singleton
9 Mischievous
10 Musical ladders
11 Complimentary close
12 Dub

13 Box, but not seriously
18 Ordinary bait
23 James who wrote "A Death in the Family"
25 Necklace ornament
26 More coquettish
28 Church law
29 Despondent comment
30 Traveled
31 Andy of the funnies
32 Region
33 Complimentary close
34 "I have the answer!"
37 Native of old China
38 Seniors' nest eggs, for short

40 1958 movie musical
41 Sired, in biblical times
43 See 46-Across
44 Chase
46 Sheik's bevy
47 Sky-blue
48 Fastballer Ryan
49 Holmes's creator
50 Place the car
51 "Night" author Wiesel
52 Diamonds or spades
56 Prefix with meter
57 ___ blind

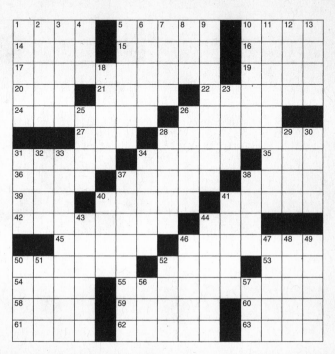

by David Levinson Wilk

38

ACROSS

1 Proficient
6 Greek promenades
11 Vestment for the clergy
14 Rival of Paris
15 Tin Woodman's quest
16 Animal house
17 "Cheyenne" star
19 Prom wear
20 Cause of strain pain
21 Musical Horne
22 Wind dir.
23 Hoosier pro
26 Fr. holy woman
29 Tourmaline, e.g.
30 Jacuzzi
31 Tones
33 "Red Roses for a Blue Lady" singer
36 Swashbuckler Flynn
40 Not a blood relative
42 Sal of song
43 "Lorna ___"
44 Turkish title of old
45 Freudian interests
47 Semiquaver, e.g.
48 "___ alive!"
50 Cone bearer
52 Voting aye
53 Meadowlark Lemon, once
59 Calif. airport
60 Fishing item
61 Military command
65 Friend of Francois
66 1982 Harrison Ford film
68 Last letter in London
69 Charlton Heston epic
70 Certain rocket engine
71 Before, to poets
72 Takes out
73 Hives

DOWN

1 St. Louis landmark
2 Welfare, with "the"
3 Arabian bigwig
4 Former Helsinki coin
5 Hauling around
6 ___ Na Na
7 "I cannot ___ lie!"
8 Like some buckets
9 Madison Square Garden and others
10 Out of cash
11 Tenochtitlan resident
12 No-goodnik
13 Kind of shorts
18 Got wet up to the ankles
24 Screen presentation
25 Hitter of 755 home runs
26 Side-wheeler, for one
27 Sushi staple
28 Congers
32 Master, in Calcutta
34 Pester
35 Up in the sky
37 Part of the mouth
38 Aware of
39 Lascivious look
41 It may rock you to sleep
46 Ravi Shankar's instrument
49 Cry in "A Streetcar Named Desire"
51 Half of a round trip
53 Shiny coating
54 More hobbled
55 Fe_2O_3, e.g.
56 Don't just stand there
57 "Golden" song
58 1966 hit "Walk Away ___"
62 Pantry pests
63 Spanish muralist
64 Son of Aphrodite
67 Sullivan and Asner

by Randall J. Hartman

ACROSS

1 Receded
6 Namesakes of 57-Down
10 "Begone!"
14 Suspect's need
15 Converted apartment
16 Time piece
17 Maugham novel made into a 1946 movie, with "The"
19 Bout of debauchery
20 Not now
21 Driver's club, for short
22 Unwanted look
24 57-Down's predecessor
25 Popular cable channel
29 Before, informally
30 Bled
31 Dernier ___
32 Worse than bad
35 Habit
37 The Man
38 Rossini opera, with "The"
41 Sailing
42 Part of Q.E.D.
43 Bottomless pit
44 Monique, e.g.: Abbr.
45 Horse's tidbit
46 Towel stitching
47 "The Amityville Horror" actress
51 Cap with a pompom
54 Ancient greetings
55 O.S.S. successor
56 Prix ___
57 Ian Fleming title
59 Facing danger
62 Wallop
63 Highlander
64 "___ ears"

65 Modern pentathlon event
66 1987 Costner role
67 What a will, e.g., may indicate?

DOWN

1 Home base, in sci-fi
2 Ennui, with "the"
3 "The Pearl Fishers" composer
4 Poet's black
5 Heading: Abbr.
6 Of an intestine
7 Film maker
8 Alphabetic run
9 Star-shaped
10 Did a blacksmith's job
11 "If I remember ___ . . ."
12 Summer time: Abbr.
13 Have a go at
18 Spinnaker, e.g.
23 Long time
25 Shade of green
26 Artist Max
27 Doctoral dread
28 WXY phone buttons
29 March instrument
32 Embarrass
33 Futile effort
34 Like many writers
35 Mary of the comics
36 Birds-feather connector
37 Fam. members
39 Transfer
40 Heraldic fur
45 "A Chorus Line" finale

46 Radiator output
48 Elicit
49 Pains' partner
50 Some strings
51 Giant
52 Skaters' jumps
53 Actress Oberon
56 Notability
57 34th Pres.
58 Agent, for short
60 Highlander's negative
61 Seinfeld, e.g.

by Mark Elliot Skolsky

40

ACROSS

1 Shortly
5 NaCl
9 Kind of cheese
14 Letterman rival
15 Wash's partner
16 Noodles
17 Traveling ice-cream seller
20 Acapulco gold
21 Active person
22 Assistants
23 Overcast
25 Denver of "The Dukes of Hazzard"
26 Fire residue
27 Gorbachev policy
31 List components
34 Press, as clothes
35 Prevaricate
36 1976 film about a Little League team
40 Oliver North's rank: Abbr.
41 Syncopated songs
42 Vast chasm
43 Getting a move on
46 Lobster eater's accessory
47 Possess
48 Outstanding athlete
52 On land
55 Not in use
56 "Honest" President
57 1958 best seller set in Southeast Asia
60 Oslo's land, on stamps
61 Scored 100 on
62 Henri's head
63 Brilliantly colored fish
64 Unites
65 Rabbit dish

DOWN

1 Choir members
2 India's first P.M.
3 Tie ___ (get smashed)
4 Yuletide beverage
5 Rushing sound
6 Yellow fever mosquito
7 Lion player of 1939
8 Capote, familiarly
9 Turns bad
10 Head of a pen
11 "Woe ___!"
12 Walk of Fame symbol
13 ___-serif (type style)
18 Ukraine port
19 Central American pyramid builders
24 Mary's pet
25 Snow-cleaning vehicles
27 One of the Allman Brothers
28 Oil of ___
29 Sexist letter start
30 Dick Tracy's love
31 Seven-year phenomenon
32 10 C-notes
33 Wriggly fish
34 Foolish
37 Utter nonsense
38 One who dips out water
39 Subsides, as the tide
44 However
45 Some T-shirts
46 Has an open wound
48 Carrying guns
49 Be silent, in music
50 Diminish in intensity
51 Ask for more Time?
52 "___ added expense"
53 Boutique
54 Wife of Zeus
55 Confront
58 Go off course
59 Part of T.G.I.F.

by Fred Piscop

ACROSS

1 Charlie Chan portrayer Warner
6 Letters after a proof
9 1908 Peace Nobelist Fredrik
14 Auger or drill
15 ___ Today
16 A McCoy, to a Hatfield
17 747 and DC-10
19 "___ which will live in infamy": F.D.R.
20 Greek earth goddess
21 British submachine gun
22 Temporary stay
26 Literally, face to face
29 Accents in "résumé"
30 Precooking solution
31 18-wheelers
32 Founder of a French dynasty
33 Meadow
34 Ninnies
35 Seeker of the Golden Fleece
36 Take ___ at (criticize)
37 Singer Kamoze
38 Spanish gent
39 "Zorba the Greek" setting
40 Genius
42 Attired for a frat party
43 Convertibles
44 Additional helpings
45 Moonshine containers
46 Phnom ___
47 Old adders
49 Nickname for DiMaggio
54 Italian bowling game
55 Record speed: Abbr.
56 Role for Valentino
57 Some sharks
58 Caribbean, e.g.
59 Circumvent

DOWN

1 Goal: Abbr.
2 Singer Rawls or Reed
3 Pitcher's pride
4 Lincoln's state: Abbr.
5 Small parachutes
6 Wicked "Snow White" figure
7 "Como ___ usted?"
8 Prosecutors, for short
9 Skedaddles
10 Like the Incas
11 "Les Miserables" protagonist
12 C.P.R. administrant
13 Deli bread
18 See 30-Down
21 Theda Bara, e.g.
22 With more attitude
23 Pacific islands, collectively
24 Single calisthenic
25 Big name in elevators
26 Gaseous mist
27 Conceptualized
28 Where oysters sleep?
30 With 18-Down, home canning items
32 ___ Major (southern constellation)
35 Army vehicles
36 35-Across's vessel
38 Cheap cigars
39 Apache chief
41 Plaster finish
42 Camp sight
44 Alabama city
46 Pontiff
47 Defense syst.
48 Feathered stole
49 Some namesakes, for short
50 Gretzky's grp.
51 Game, in France
52 Ending with human or planet
53 Supplement, with "out"

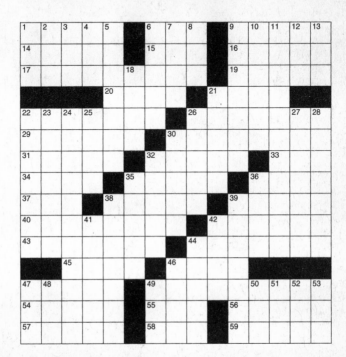

by Dean Niles

42

ACROSS

1 Brighton pub
6 Retreat
10 Pull an all-nighter
14 Mitchell family name
15 One, to Wilhelm
16 Proctor & Gamble soap
17 Like an inner tube, geometrically
18 Catch
19 Kind of rock
20 Lo-o-o-ong efforts from a QB?
23 It must be followed
24 Hot times on the Riviera
25 It runs up trees
28 Computer adjunct
30 Jack of clubs, in cards
33 Geographical datum
35 Early baby word
36 One who's practical and tidy, they say
38 Switches receivers?
42 Tin can's target
43 60's singer Little ___
44 Memorable New York Met Tommie
45 Prospector's need
46 Pompous pronoun
50 Minerva, symbolically
51 Coin catalogue rating
52 Swamp thing
54 Navy's anti-Army strategy?
60 Betting sum
61 Suffix with switch
62 More foxy
63 Teen Beat cover subject
64 Ivy League power
65 Floor worker
66 Address with ZIP code 10001: Abbr.
67 Elder or alder
68 Pimlico garb

DOWN

1 Sen. Trent
2 Cry of excitement
3 N.F.L. co-founder Joe
4 Constellation near Perseus
5 Prepare to tie shoes
6 Envoy's assignment
7 Open to breezes
8 Peeved
9 Payback
10 Teacher's charge
11 Word with arms or foot
12 Hertz rival
13 Daft
21 Gloomy tune
22 Do one's duty
25 Became alert
26 Island NE of Maracaibo
27 He was called "El Líder"
29 Bumps
30 Polite Italian word
31 Discredited Veep
32 Fashion figure
34 Alicia of "Falcon Crest"
37 Tax-deferred plan, for short
39 Uncomplaining
40 Burnt, or practically so
41 Man's man
47 Broken, as promises
48 Parent
49 Luaus
51 Bad move
53 CCCXXVI doubled
54 Good wine quality
55 Screwball
56 ___ of the above
57 Hunter's take
58 Onion's kin
59 Misreckons
60 Hem holder

by Fran and Lou Sabin

ACROSS

1 One-named supermodel
5 Ready and willing's partner
9 One praised in Mecca
14 Attorney General Janet
15 Paris's Rue de la ___
16 French valley
17 Tiny tunnelers
18 Ingrid's "Casablanca" role
19 Not evenly padded, as a mattress
20 Like an animal . . .
23 Historical period
24 Use a crowbar
25 Cream puff, for one
29 Miles per hour, e.g.
31 At the present
34 In the future
35 O. Henry's "The Gift of the ___"
36 ___ Gigio (frequent Ed Sullivan guest)
37 . . . vegetable . . .
40 Pulled to pieces
41 Ontario tribe
42 Blabs
43 Muddy home
44 The former Mrs. Bono
45 Better than better
46 Texas patriot Houston
47 Buddy
48 . . . or mineral
55 Assign, as a portion
57 Polly, to Tom Sawyer
58 "The Andy Griffith Show" role
59 River by the Louvre
60 Manuscript encl.
61 What a cowboy calls a lady
62 Flute player
63 New World abbr.
64 Alka-Seltzer sound

DOWN

1 Mideast hot spot
2 Bill of fare
3 The "A" of ABM
4 Pinocchio's giveaway
5 Bee colony
6 Light wood
7 One of "The Simpsons"
8 Test
9 Magnetism
10 Stinky
11 7-Up ingredient
12 Dadaist Hans
13 "Yo!"
21 ___ cotta
22 Of the eye
25 Treaties
26 "The game is ___": Holmes
27 Tale
28 Prefix with photo or phone
29 Indy entrant
30 Tropical fever
31 Lofty
32 Foreign-made General Motors cars
33 Deserving the booby prize
35 Stallion's mate
36 Federal agents, informally
38 Noodlehead
39 New York city
44 Reagan's predecessor
45 Speed demon's cry
46 Precious ___
47 Parson's home
48 Accident on ice
49 "The Right Stuff" org.
50 U.S. Pacific territory
51 Frolic
52 October gem
53 "See you," in Sorrento
54 1996 running mate
55 Nile viper
56 Maui garland

by Stephanie Spadaccini

44

ACROSS

1 Bushy coif
5 Belle or Bart
10 "Dancing Queen" pop group
14 It goes with runners
15 Army Corps of Engineers construction
16 Burrow
17 In direct competition
19 Mid 12th-century date
20 Long fish
21 Rich Little, e.g.
22 Drew out
24 Three-sided sword
25 Savage
26 One of the Greats
29 Half step, in music
32 Partner of ways
33 Shack
34 Corn crib
35 Early Andean
36 More rational
37 Diplomat's skill
38 Fr. holy woman
39 Burger King, to McDonald's
40 Where the loot gets left
41 Autumn drink
43 Crave, with "for"
44 "You Must Remember This" author
45 Kennel cry
46 Browning automatics
48 Effrontery
49 Menlo Park initials
52 Shut noisily
53 Kind of combat
56 Gambling, e.g.
57 ___ orange

58 Mitch Miller's instrument
59 Squint
60 Firefighting need
61 Old TV detective Peter

DOWN

1 Connors defeater, 1975
2 Hightail it
3 Not imagined
4 Roulette bet
5 Inclined
6 Snicker
7 Say it's so
8 New Deal proj.
9 Jesus Christ, with "the"
10 Virtually
11 One after the other
12 Ill temper
13 Saharan
18 Uses a camcorder
23 Resort near Copper Mountain
24 Soprano Berger
25 Angle on a gem
26 Plain People
27 Slowly, in music
28 In-person, as an interview
29 Sub detector
30 Recess
31 Computer command
33 Wealthy ones
36 Two-headed lady exhibit, e.g.
37 Part of L.S.T.
39 Liturgy
40 Film producer Ponti
42 More tranquil
43 Horse restraint

45 Sheriff's star, e.g.
46 Invitation letters
47 Tennis's Nastase
48 Pesky insect
49 No-no: Var.
50 Erelong
51 First place
54 Simile center
55 Not a sharer

by Gregory E. Paul

ACROSS

1 Bankrolls
5 Gumbo vegetable
9 Military group
14 Take on
15 "Gallipoli" director
16 Mozart offering
17 Start of a quote by 39-Across
20 Old schoolhouse item
21 Nostradamus, e.g.
22 Where the worm turns
23 Geisha's garment
25 Droop
27 Function
28 Record producer Brian
29 ___-ran
32 Noble's partner
34 Tear asunder
36 Tombstone lawman
38 Comedian Foxx
39 See 17-Across
42 Open a bit
44 Rock music's Ford
45 Trans World Dome team
49 Like a harvest moon
51 Popular race
53 The pause that refreshes?
54 Fish cookout
55 Sweet potato
57 Radio antenna
59 Folder's locale
61 Gilbert of "Roseanne"
64 John Lennon hit
65 End of the quote
68 Where the buffalo roam
69 Town in Nevada
70 Otherwise
71 Single-masted vessel
72 Audition for a part
73 Textile worker

DOWN

1 Narrow margin of victory
2 Carrier
3 "Get real!"
4 Former defense collective
5 Bird of prey
6 Ivories and others
7 Get carried away?
8 One born on April 1
9 Debate side
10 Chooses
11 Echo
12 Exalted
13 "Lone Star" director John
18 Singer Horne
19 Colorless
24 Designer Cassini
26 Actress with a "Tootsie" role
30 Spinnaker or jib
31 Satellite's path
33 Bring up
35 Actress Cannon
37 Gov. Wilson
40 Bacchanalian event
41 Money in Johannesburg
42 Advent
43 He's on "Tonight" tonight
46 Irregularity
47 Lethargic feeling
48 Not a saver
49 Auction bids
50 Daybreak direction
52 New Zealander
56 "Politically Incorrect" host Bill
58 Sat (for)
60 Proof word
62 Provoke
63 "Lonely Boy" singer
66 Slangy affirmative
67 The Eternal

by Michael W. Perry

46

ACROSS
1 Spring
5 Upper-story room
10 Ali who said "Open sesame!"
14 Latin journey
15 Material for uniforms
16 Arab prince
17 Plot size
18 "Greetings!"
19 Suffix with million
20 Chickens that lay brown eggs
23 Toward shelter
24 Old French coin
25 Mad ___ (Wonderland character)
28 Pedaler's place
33 Kitchen garment
34 Interstate hauler
35 Actress Myrna
36 Attraction for winter vacationers in the South
40 ___ Aviv
41 Followers: Suffix
42 ___ the Barbarian
43 Soup crackers
46 ___ Anderson of TV's "Baywatch"
47 Half of dos
48 Play part
49 Easy-gaited saddle horse
57 Pitcher Nolan
58 Bridal walkway
59 Not for
60 "Rule Britannia" composer
61 Like certain dentures
62 Tide type
63 Ground grain
64 Snoozes
65 Remove, in editing

DOWN
1 Pinocchio, at times
2 Make art on glass
3 Pertaining to aircraft
4 Lion or coyote
5 Sorer
6 "One of ___ days, Alice . . ."
7 Money drawer
8 1985 movie "To Live and Die ___"
9 Kind of cap
10 Face hardship bravely
11 She's a sweetie in Tahiti
12 Wren or hen
13 Greek Mars
21 1985 Nicholas Gage best seller
22 Buck's mate
25 Sword handles
26 Cop ___ (negotiate for a lighter sentence)
27 Folklore dwarf
28 Defeats
29 Radio host Don
30 Skirt type
31 Having a key, in music
32 "Laughing" animal
34 Encl. for a reply
37 Jurassic Park revival
38 La ___ opera house
39 One's birthplace
44 Burrow
45 Ending with nectar or saturn
46 ___ that be
48 Rent again
49 Mine vehicle
50 Jane who loved Mr. Rochester
51 Zola novel
52 Ex-Cleveland QB Brian
53 Intuitive feelings
54 Where the patella is
55 And others: Abbr.
56 Properly aged

by Sally Jo Walther

ACROSS

1. ___ blocker
5. Cabbie
9. Desert flora
14. Latin 101 word
15. Cousin of a Tony
16. Autumn color
17. Singer McEntire
18. Give the slip to
19. Squirrel away
20. Alien art form, some say
23. Magnum and others, for short
24. Give it ___ (try)
25. "Now, about . . ."
26. Getaways
28. Hilton Head Island, for one
30. Prohibitionists would like to prohibit it
33. Caught but good
36. Danish money
37. Agreement
40. Interrupt, as a dancer
42. Parroted
43. Fitzgerald and others
45. Bee and snake products
47. Boo-boos
49. Turkey moistener
53. Cartoon skunk ___ Le Pew
54. TV ad
56. "Norma ___"
57. SASE, e.g.
59. Fruit pastry
62. Ravel work, with "La"
64. Legal scholar Guinier
65. Villa d'___
66. "Give peace ___ time, O Lord": Morning Prayer
67. Prime time hour
68. Mets stadium
69. Gently gallops
70. Pub round
71. Like a Granny Smith apple

DOWN

1. Where train commuters drink
2. Come to the fore
3. No-nos
4. Pronto!
5. Kind of medicine
6. Call off a takeoff
7. 50's western "The ___ Kid"
8. Ship's central beam
9. Russian horseman
10. Take steps
11. Auto disassembly site
12. Actress Hatcher
13. Gets one's goat
21. Singer Irene
22. Building wing
27. Quagmire
29. Recorded
30. Point after deuce
31. Single
32. Conducted
34. Disposable diaper brand
35. Bordeaux summer
37. Foot: Lat.
38. The works
39. Carriage horse sound
41. People who don't count
44. Evening meals
46. ___ Hari
48. Each
50. Country singer Yearwood
51. Resurrection Mass day
52. Warm up again
54. Escargot
55. Tubular pasta
57. Stephen King topic
58. Prefix with second
60. Arm bone
61. Hornets' home
63. Take to court

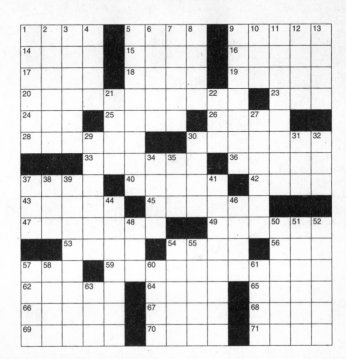

by Elizabeth C. Gorski

48

ACROSS

1 Garden dweller
5 Cassius and company, in "Julius Caesar"
10 Achievement
14 Prefix with byte or buck
15 Run with a hon?
16 Site of the MGM Grand
17 December 25 activity
20 Severe
21 These may get a welcome sight
22 Pick apart
24 Hereabout
25 ___-relief
28 Creeks
30 Drafted
34 "What's the ___?"
35 Court org.
37 Wee bit
38 Convivial holiday affair
42 Pub needs
43 Positions
44 Part of TNT
45 Like Clifford Odets's "Waiting for Lefty"
48 "Whip It" rock group
49 Smoke signal message, maybe
50 Kind of bond
52 Baltic port
54 Used a caret-and-stick approach?
58 Pinpoint
62 Sign-off a la Clement Moore
64 Nefariousness
65 Opposite of viejo
66 Campus V.I.P.
67 ___ fide (bad faith)
68 Bit of parsley
69 Bristle

DOWN

1 Sheriff Tupper of "Murder, She Wrote"
2 Agric. or H.H.S., e.g.
3 Ripener
4 Frenzied
5 Political moderate
6 School subj.
7 Hits, in slang
8 Stage extension
9 Looked lasciviously
10 Unlimited choice
11 Counting-out word
12 Add to the pot
13 Play horseshoes
18 Mythical flier
19 Scorch
23 Oasis trees
25 British swaggerer
26 Pale
27 Maestro Koussevitzky
29 Sedate
31 Habits
32 In ___ (not yet born)
33 Golden apple bestower
36 Daisylike bloom
39 Patron of Columbus
40 Marine, informally
41 Equiangular geometrical shape
46 Sagan of "Cosmos"
47 Certain missiles
51 Mounter's assist
53 These can be citric
54 Gossip tidbit
55 Suddenly bright star
56 Spinnaker, e.g.
57 Active one
59 1957 Pulitzer winner
60 "___ does it!"
61 Sicilian sight
63 Egg: Prefix

by Nancy S. Ross

ACROSS

1 Wood-turning tool
6 Welcome smell
11 Undergrad degrees
14 Disney mermaid
15 Site of golfing's Blue Monster
16 Genetic trait carrier
17 Make an error
19 Consume
20 Part to play
21 Teacher in a turban
23 Conciliate
27 Gotten back, as land in battle
29 Villain
30 Capital of Tasmania
31 Welles of "Citizen Kane"
32 Golden Horde member
33 Premium cable channel
36 Diana of the Supremes
37 Munchhausen's title
38 Lima, e.g.
39 Suffix with superintend
40 Rubbernecker
41 Fanny ___ of the Ziegfeld Follies
42 Area of Manhattan
44 Lighthouse light
45 Artist's studio
47 Make manhattans and such
48 Ear parts
49 Is up
50 Zoo bird
51 Be outrageous
58 ___ room
59 Deceive
60 Charge

61 "For shame!"
62 Mystery writer's award
63 Nairobi's land

DOWN

1 Terhune's "___: a Dog"
2 Opposite of "Dep." on a flight board
3 Tijuana uncle
4 With it, 40's-style
5 It loops the Loop
6 Dancer Astaire
7 Caftan
8 ". . . man ___ mouse?"
9 ___ de mer
10 Selected athlete
11 Get a party going
12 "What's in ___?"
13 Luxurious sheet material
18 Hydrant hookup
22 Card game for two
23 Dean Martin song subject
24 Juan of Argentina
25 Not take responsibility
26 1961 space chimp
27 Copter part
28 Israeli statesman Abba
30 Quarters in a sultan's palace
32 Grow narrower
34 Breakfast sizzler
35 Upturned, as a box
37 Cotton bundle
38 Baby sitter's nightmare
40 Chewy part of meat
41 Bananas
43 Hearty drink
44 Alternative to a shower
45 With ears pricked
46 Weighty books
47 Ulan ___, Mongolia
49 ___ carotene
52 Help
53 Beer barrel
54 Feed lines to
55 Massachusetts cape
56 Braggart knight of the Round Table
57 H, to Greeks

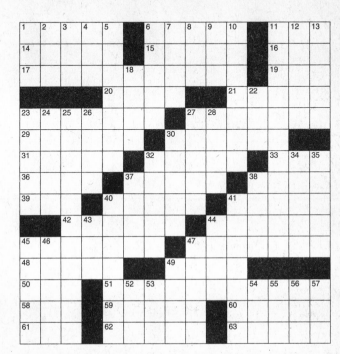

by C. F. Murray

50

ACROSS

1. Slam-dunks
5. Stiller and ___
10. Prefix with business
14. Like Nash's lama
15. Waters of song
16. Amorphous mass
17. 1935 Cole Porter song
20. Pundit
21. Olio
22. Disney's "___ and the Detectives"
25. Vietnam's Ngo ___ Diem
26. No longer hold up
29. F. Scott Fitzgerald had one: Abbr.
31. New York's ___ Island
35. Swellhead's problem
36. Number of mousquetaires
38. Invited
39. Unofficial Australian "anthem"
43. Anon's partner
44. ___ objection (go along)
45. Nurse's bag
46. Lax
49. Garden tool
50. Molly Bloom's last word in "Ulysses"
51. Pot builder
53. Torture chamber item
55. Well-to-do
59. Gut-wrenching feeling
63. 1939 Andrews Sisters hit
66. ___ ideal (perfect model)
67. "Camelot" tunesmith
68. Mariner Ericson
69. Memo abbr.
70. Winter hazard
71. Advanced

DOWN

1. Steven of Apple computers
2. Once more
3. Prefix with phone
4. Ooze
5. Encountered
6. Biblical verb ending
7. "Beg your pardon"
8. Bridge action
9. One of the Carringtons, on "Dynasty"
10. Largest of the United Arab Emirates
11. Fluent
12. Author Jaffe
13. "___ to differ!"
18. Pacific Fleet admiral of W.W. II
19. Lady's partner
23. Letters from Calvary
24. Den fathers
26. Drain
27. Century plant
28. Automaton
30. Go-getter
32. Loquacious
33. Jockey Arcaro
34. ___-foot oil
37. Daub
40. Demonstration test
41. Singer Paul
42. Cobbler's tip
47. Slight
48. Base runner's stat
52. Register
54. Small hill
55. "Dancing Queen" pop group
56. Podiatrists' concerns
57. Potential Guinness Book entry
58. Shade giver
60. Open delight
61. Scrape, as the knee
62. Electee of 1908
64. Female with a wool coat
65. Tennis call

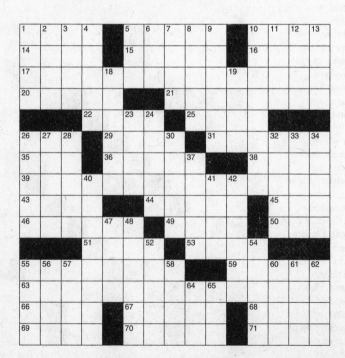

by Arthur S. Verdesca

ACROSS

1 Thermonuclear blast maker
6 Trot or canter
10 "Listen!"
14 Golfer Palmer, informally
15 Killer whale
16 Place to put a thimble
17 Corporate recruiter
19 "Mama" speaker
20 Wheat or barley covering
21 Wild time
22 Sty
24 Sty animals
25 Identical
26 Quiet spot to sit
29 September birthstone
33 Market price
34 Treadmill unit
35 Keats pieces
36 Lemon and orange drinks
37 Like some renewable energy
38 ___ moss
39 Gin flavor
40 Thigh muscle, for short
41 Garden tool
42 Long workday, perhaps
44 ___ Pieces
45 Lena or Ken of film
46 Violinist Leopold
47 Philadelphia N.F.L.'ers
50 Book before Romans
51 Disputed skill, for short
54 Didn't have traction
55 Snob
58 Fishing need

59 Buffalo's county
60 Jonah's swallower
61 Not far
62 Cub Scout groups
63 Besmirch

DOWN

1 Response to a comic
2 Make beer, e.g.
3 ___ even keel
4 ___-Atlantic
5 Serve well
6 Deep bells
7 Pretentious
8 Freezer stuff
9 Roofing material
10 Crop-dusting plane
11 Surmounting
12 "First in, first out," e.g.

13 Pottery oven
18 Impulse
23 Mischievous sort
24 Census taker's target
25 Meal gotten from a garden
26 "Stop!," to Popeye
27 Soup scoop
28 60's–70's Mets star ___ Jones
29 Marner of fiction
30 Think tank products
31 "The Cloister and the Hearth" author
32 ___ Park, Colo.
34 Grieve
37 Stepped on, as a bug
41 Goes up and down

43 ___ Miss
44 Buzzi of "Laugh-In"
46 Partner of pains
47 "SportsCenter" channel
48 Ingredient in facial tissues
49 ___ monster
50 Opposed to, hillbilly-style
51 And others: Abbr.
52 Unload, on Wall Street
53 Zebras, to lions
56 Ill temper
57 Wed. follower

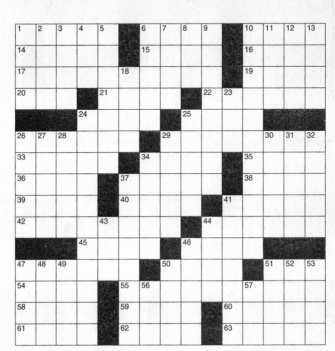

by Gregory E. Paul

52

ACROSS

1 Snacks in shells
6 Panty raid site
10 Quartet on a baseball field
14 First Hebrew letter
15 "Zip-___-Doo-Dah"
16 Mosaic piece
17 Bulldogger's event
18 "Oh, my aching head!," e.g.
19 Big chemical company
20 Movie with a hard-to-rhyme name
23 In a funk
24 Ages and ages
25 Midafternoon, on a sundial
26 Some E.R. cases
27 Black-eye soothers
32 Bump off
35 Demagnetize, as a tape
36 Shoebox letters
37 King with a hard-to-rhyme name
41 Suffix with hero
42 "Crazy" singer Patsy
43 "___ Wonderful Life"
44 Reaches the wrong party
46 Kind of dance or bride
48 Old biddy
49 1/24 case
50 Take steps
53 Pirate with a hard-to-rhyme name
58 Boor
59 It may get a licking after dinner
60 Wavelike design
61 Nave neighbor
62 Links carrier
63 "Stormy Weather" composer
64 Herbicide target
65 Proposer's prop
66 Most trifling

DOWN

1 Bite-size pies
2 Hello from Ho
3 Handed over
4 Crude cartel
5 Chased away
6 Runyon or Wayans
7 Bad whiff
8 Bring in
9 28-Down handout
10 Ideal spot
11 Pipe-smoking former Congresswoman Fenwick
12 Ballet bend
13 D.C. V.I.P.
21 ___ Altos, Calif.
22 Not so green
26 Olive of "Thimble Theatre"
27 Shackles
28 See 9-Down
29 Anka's "___ Beso"
30 Toga party needs
31 "Did you ever ___ lassie...?"
32 Triathlon leg
33 Actress Virna ___
34 Home to the down-and-out
35 Pianist Gilels
38 Cupcake topper
39 Part of a recipe title
40 Televise
45 In need of body work
46 Used to be
47 Kind of magnetism
49 100 smackers
50 St. Teresa's birthplace
51 First known asteroid
52 Lott of Mississippi
53 Run easily
54 Bookworm's counterpart
55 Algerian port
56 Roll call call
57 Tribal tales
58 Corpus juris

by Fred Piscop

ACROSS

1 Dilemma features, figuratively
6 Take measures
9 Starbucks offering
14 Up's partner
15 London facility
16 Pierre's girlfriends
17 With 37- and 61-Across, a 1936 title
20 Monogram of '52 and '56
21 Crumb
22 Prohibited
23 Rap sheet items
25 Amenhotep IV's god
26 Florida city, informally
29 Rockies' div.
31 Script ending
32 Author of 17-, 37- and 61-Across
34 Borodin's "Prince ___"
36 1995 Stallone title role
37 See 17-Across
39 Ephesus' land
42 Take down ___
44 Category of 17-, 37- and 61-Across
46 Reunion grp.
48 Woman in Fitzgerald's "Tender Is the Night"
50 ___ Stanley Gardner
51 Mont Blanc, e.g.
53 After-hours job, maybe
55 Be confident of
57 Really bad coffee
58 ___ soda
61 See 17-Across

64 "___ as I can see . . ."
65 Antipollution org.
66 Injun Joe creator
67 "___ It" (1983 Tom Cruise film)
68 Wasn't active
69 Brief brawl

DOWN

1 "Very funny!"
2 Reed section member
3 Spreadsheet components
4 Weirdo
5 An acoustic guitarist may use one
6 European carrier
7 Bamboozle
8 Peanut brittle base
9 Retreat
10 Amorphous critter
11 Singer born Anna Mae Bullock
12 Hay spreader
13 Dead Sea Scrolls scribe
18 Dry, in a way
19 Martini & ___
23 Supermarket chain
24 "Benson" actress
26 Three before E
27 Galley need
28 Easy questions, so to speak
30 Cry of relief
33 Shangri-La
35 Aaher's partner

38 Salami or bologna
40 Taken ___
41 Copy
43 Popular toy since 1964
45 Relax
46 Beauty parlor treatment
47 "The Tempest" king
49 Film festival site
52 Zhou ___
54 "Golden Boy" playwright
56 Go sour
58 Petty quarrel
59 Touched down
60 Late-night name
62 Busy bee in Apr.
63 Be light, in poker

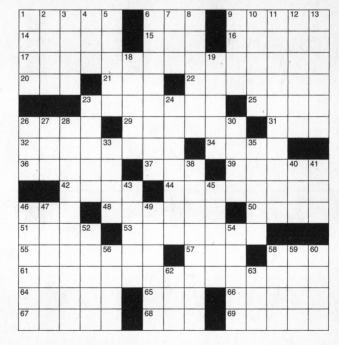

by Charles E. Gersch

ACROSS

1 Grab
6 Wood strip used as a bed support
10 Talented
14 Indiana basketballer
15 Munich Mister
16 Vast emptiness
17 Sports facility
18 "___ bitten, twice shy"
19 Opposer
20 Finally understood
23 Cat with a bowl of milk, e.g.
27 Medicinal plants
28 Singer Guthrie
29 Revolutionary War firearm
34 Makes level
36 Sidewalk material
37 Owns
40 Ocean predator
43 Needle part
44 Put down forcibly
45 Kingdom in the South Seas
46 Imaginary
48 ___ canal
49 Open-mouthed
53 Set aflame
55 One who can have you going around in circles?
60 Created
61 Affirm positively
62 Artist's prop
67 Notion
68 What you might be in when you're out
69 Crème de la crème
70 Midterm, say
71 Pool exercise
72 "Saturday Night Fever" music

DOWN

1 Resort
2 A barber might nick it
3 Winter road hazard
4 Kind of Buddhism
5 Delete
6 Film or play
7 Loaned
8 Keystone place
9 Shade giver
10 Be of use
11 Drum played with the hands
12 Like a ballerina's body
13 Revises, as copy
21 Sleeve's contents
22 Most recent
23 Wood shop machine
24 Set out for display
25 Showy feather
26 Robert Frost writing
30 Wedding helper
31 Commemorative marker
32 Australian "bear"
33 Finish
35 Part two
37 Vietnam's capital
38 Specialized vocabulary
39 Rollerblade, e.g.
41 What computer programs do
42 Taxi feature
47 Prevaricate
49 Allow in
50 A+ or C–
51 Helpers
52 Skirt fold
54 Monopolist's trait
56 British raincoats
57 State openly
58 Tractor-trailer
59 Cable car
63 Boxer Muhammad
64 Female sib
65 And so forth
66 Virgo's predecessor

by Nancy Kavanaugh

ACROSS

1 G.I.'s lullaby?
5 Forty-niner's filing
10 Visually dull
14 Mate's shout
15 Barbera's partner in cartooning
16 Go backpacking
17 Worrier's habit
19 Hillside shelter
20 Oscar winner Sophia
21 Kramden's pal on "The Honeymooners"
23 Hot and dry
26 Sending to one's fate
27 Language of the Koran
28 French novelist Honoré de ___
29 Salome's seven
30 Aladdin's enabler
31 Vladimir Putin's onetime org.
34 French 101 verb
35 Redhead's dye
36 Gin flavoring
37 ___ Bingle (Crosby moniker)
38 Toss back and forth
39 Begins to flutter the eyelids
40 Shuttle plane
42 Jolson's river of song
43 Noted Parthenon sculptor
45 In the middle of
46 Small wound
47 Drink for Dracula
48 Mélange
49 Amazing to behold
54 Small amount of milk
55 Rent out again
56 Met song
57 Gets soaked
58 Up to one's ears
59 TelePrompTer display

DOWN

1 "The Joy Luck Club" author
2 "Caught you!"
3 Taro dish
4 One of 17 in a haiku
5 French president Jacques
6 Head toward evening
7 Have ___ (be connected)
8 Quaint lodging
9 Mississippi's state tree
10 TV's "___ and Greg"
11 Highly amusing
12 Ohio tire center
13 Living thing
18 Mussorgsky's Godunov
22 Move like molasses
23 "___ by the bell!"
24 Mountain ridge
25 Like a horror movie
26 Actor DeVito
28 Diver's dread, with "the"
30 Ranking above species
32 Tennessee political family
33 Assailed on all sides
35 "Carmen" highlight
36 Hold one's ground
38 Vivacity
39 Attack like an eagle
41 Cementheads
42 Not chunky, as peanut butter
43 Raindrop sounds
44 Sun: Prefix
45 Suisse range
47 Horror icon Lugosi
50 Archery wood
51 High dudgeon
52 Put the kibosh on
53 Gangster's gun

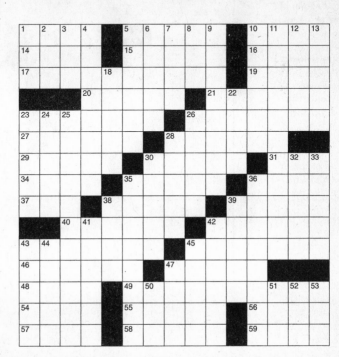

by Frances Hansen

ACROSS

1 Low-lying area
6 Dept. of Labor grp.
10 A&P part: Abbr.
13 "Three's Company" actress
15 Dazzles
16 River inlet
17 Start of a quip
20 English maritime county
21 Core
22 Matterhorn, e.g.: Abbr.
23 Reason for imprisonment, once
25 Satyr's kin
26 Prettify oneself
29 War room items
31 Recipe amts.
32 Not participate
34 Beauty's admirer
36 Part 2 of the quip
40 Covalent bond formers
41 Like firewater
43 One of Henry's Catherines
46 Concrete
48 Irritated moods
49 Meg's "Prelude to a Kiss" co-star
50 I-80 et al.
52 Stat that's good when it's low
53 Sony rival
56 Beethoven's "Pathétique," e.g.
59 End of the quip
62 Follower of Christ?
63 Eighty Eight, for one
64 Nero's tutor
65 N.J. clock setting
66 Tammany skewerer
67 Radiation quantities

DOWN

1 St. Louis-to-Little Rock dir.
2 Carpenter's finishing touch
3 Ancient resident of Jordan's present-day capital
4 Wanton look
5 Coastal raptors
6 Symbol of might
7 Fragrant climbing plant
8 Pianist Myra
9 [No return allowed]
10 Scenes of action
11 1996 golf movie
12 Gets dark
14 It has runners
18 Bit of gossip

19 No-no at some intersections
22 G.I. constabulary
24 Played the nanny
27 Saudi Arabia is one
28 Any miniature golf shot
30 Talk trash to
33 Son of Odin
35 Transporters since '76
37 Beryl varieties
38 Halves
39 Hypnotize
42 Fed. management agcy.
43 Flat peppermint candy
44 Warm hellos
45 Take offense at
47 More, in a saying

51 Dipsos
54 It may be pumped
55 Gymnastics coach Karolyi
57 Cry out for
58 ___ Domini
60 Musician's suffix
61 Jabber

by Gene Newman

ACROSS

1 Old Russian leader
5 Hogwash
10 Dressed
14 Early political caucus state
15 Land divided at the 38th parallel
16 Letterman rival
17 Al-___ (valuable support group)
18 Tehran native
19 Hint of things to come
20 Venerable public servant
23 Sharp
24 Timothy who took trips
25 Frankie of "Beach Blanket Bingo"
28 The "E" in Q.E.D.
30 Fish's breathing organ
31 Occurring involuntarily
36 Three ___ match
37 Children's card game
39 "___ Got a Secret"
40 "Burr" author
42 Search, as the horizon
43 Who, what or where sentence: Abbr.
44 Presentable
46 Capital of South 15-Across
49 Stubborn as ___
51 Coleridge character
56 Lay ___ the line
57 Give a speech
58 Verve
60 Verne captain
61 Führer's followers
62 Puerto ___
63 "Jurassic Park" terror
64 Big tournaments
65 Tibetan beasts

DOWN

1 Grp. with informants
2 Area
3 One who's off base, maybe
4 Klugman's co-star in 70's TV
5 Slope for slaloming
6 Least desirable
7 Angry
8 Horne or Olin
9 Café au ___
10 Near
11 Auxiliary proposition, in math
12 Lend ___ (listen)
13 An Osmond
21 Prefix with system or sphere
22 Endangered antelope
25 Intensely interested
26 In ___ veritas
27 Banned orchard chemical
28 And others: Abbr.
29 Louis XIV, e.g.
31 Does sums
32 Thurman of "The Avengers"
33 Cheese nibblers
34 A "terrible" 1-Across
35 Penny
37 Rudimentary seed
38 Tell whoppers
41 March 21 occurrence
42 Overlook's offering
44 Coercion
45 Yale student
46 Benevolent one
47 Go in
48 Entreaty to "all ye faithful"
49 Wow
50 Morning, in Montmartre
52 Unacceptable act
53 Links hazard
54 Charles Lamb's pseudonym
55 Torture device
59 Phone book listings: Abbr.

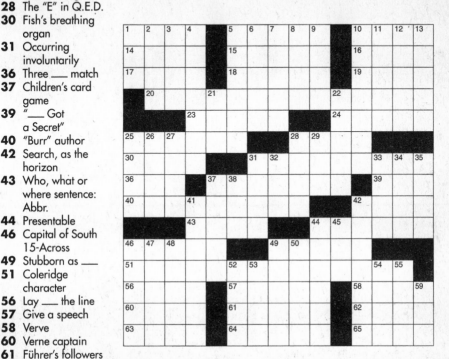

by Randy Sowell

58

ACROSS

1 One of the worlds in "The War of the Worlds"
5 Baby's first word, maybe
9 Designer Donna
14 Touch on
15 PC pic
16 Alpha's opposite
17 Kennedy matriarch
18 The N.F.L.'s Aikman
19 Dentist's request
20 Start of a quip
22 Stuffed bear
23 Cache
24 Final approval
28 Quip, part 2
34 Paul Simon's "Slip __ Away"
38 Form of evidence, these days
39 Frankfurt's river
40 Crescent shapes: Var.
41 Skill
43 Word for Yorick
44 Stars and Stripes land
47 Compassionate
48 End of the quip
51 Verso's opposite
52 Ancient Greek colony
57 Mrs. Gorbachev
61 Speaker of the quip
63 Cockeyed
64 Gyro meat
66 Prefix with second
67 Cubic meter
68 Devil's doing
69 Town on the Thames
70 Model at work
71 Like Marilyn Monroe
72 Learning the times table, e.g.

DOWN

1 Home run champ until 1998
2 Up's partner
3 Rene of "Tin Cup"
4 Beef on the hoof
5 Catcher's need
6 Unlike this answer
7 Jersey greeting?
8 "__ luck?"
9 Bow and scrape
10 Grenoble girlfriend
11 Foxx of "Sanford and Son"
12 Like fine wine
13 Word before "a soul"
21 Ledger entry
25 "Then what?"
26 Hither's partner
27 Wrap in bandages
29 Make certain
30 1947 Oscar winner Celeste
31 Light bulb, figuratively
32 Chattanooga's home: Abbr.
33 One-named designer
34 Meat loaf serving
35 Lollapalooza
36 __ the finish
37 Half a 50's sitcom couple
42 Decorated Murphy
45 [not my error]
46 Toward the rear
49 Cash register part
50 Star of silent oaters
53 Title holder
54 "Rad!"
55 Comeback in a kids' argument
56 Make amends
57 Coarse file
58 Concerning
59 Alibi __ (excuse makers)
60 Withered
62 With adroitness
64 "__ Miz"
65 Forum greeting

by Dorothy E. Donaldson

ACROSS

1 Windshield sticker
6 Employee's move, for short
10 Cries heard around cute babies
13 Dupe
14 Quark's place
15 Headlight setting
16 Spotted wildcat
17 Loafers don't grow on this
19 Musical markings don't grow on this
21 Oscar winner Davis
22 Ceiling spinner
23 Mileage rating org.
24 Supermarket checkout item
26 Cupid, to the Greeks
28 Hiker's route
30 "Try me" preceder
31 Clears of vermin
34 Slip through the cracks
36 It might make you see things
37 Baby fowl don't grow on this
40 Accomplished
43 Pennsylvania port
44 Like a wake-up time on an alarm clock
48 "___ first you don't..."
50 Pulls the plug on
52 "Comin' ___ the Rye"
53 Obsolescent term of address
55 Confucian truth
58 Dawn goddess
59 Deadly snake
60 Morays don't grow on this
62 Henhouse products don't grow on this
65 QB Doug
66 Maiden name preceder
67 Plane measure
68 Like horses at blacksmiths
69 Ave. crossers
70 Bastes
71 Krupp Works city

DOWN

1 "I do ___!"
2 1930's first lady
3 Kind of film
4 Pueblo brick
5 Abate
6 Too hasty
7 Addis Ababa's land: Abbr.
8 John, to Ringo
9 Certain sorority girl
10 Kind of gland
11 Ballpark purchases
12 Slung mud at
13 Tipped, as a hat
18 Watch
20 Chucklehead
24 Meat-and-vegetables fare
25 Canary's call
27 Midwest Indian
29 Appealed
32 Everyday article
33 Fathered
35 According to
38 Motion picture
39 N.Y.P.D. investigator
40 Devil
41 "Hmmm, it's not coming to me"
42 Compensation in a lawsuit
45 Protect in a cover
46 Shoreline problem
47 Deep-sixed
49 Dancer's woe
51 Sault ___ Marie
54 Shoreline shower
56 Actress Woodard
57 Gawks at
60 Hellenic H's
61 "tom thumb" star Tamblyn
63 Live and breathe
64 Just out

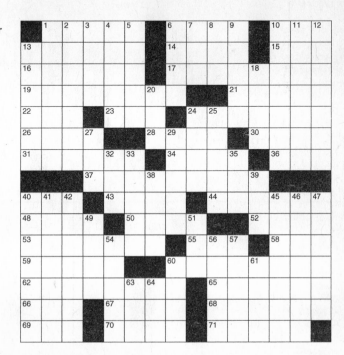

by Fred Piscop

ACROSS

1 Itsy-bitsy
4 Jerks
9 Mob
14 Ewe's mate
15 Field of play
16 Easy-to-carry instruments
17 Part of an octopus
18 Not now
19 Harass
20 What Rick Blaine never said
23 Endings for hydrocarbons
24 Bambi's mother, e.g.
25 Ordered (around)
28 Leopold and ___ (big 1920's murder case)
30 Wharton degree
33 Semester's-end events
34 Robe for Caesar
35 Hardly a genius
36 One-man show about President Truman
39 Yemeni port
40 Simplify
41 Signs to beware of
42 Beatty or Rorem
43 ___ and sciences
44 High-priced furs
45 ___ Baba
46 Prefix with plane
47 Plaintive plea in the 1919 Black Sox scandal
54 It makes a clicking noise
55 Tony winner ___ Lenya
56 Before, for a bard
57 Actor John of "The Addams Family"
58 Dutch painter Jan
59 ___ Aviv

60 Places for hinges
61 Where to find dates?
62 Message in a bottle?

DOWN

1 Coat or shawl
2 Rank below marquis
3 Austen heroine
4 Certain Indonesians
5 Speechified
6 Followers of epsilons
7 Force on Earth: Abbr.
8 "Nobody doesn't like ___ Lee"
9 Schmooze (with)
10 Overly overweight
11 Parks on a bus

12 Consider
13 N.Y.C. clock setting
21 Toadies
22 Rating a 10
25 Commenced
26 Rust, for one
27 Put in the bank
28 Fertile soil
29 Look like a wolf?
30 Mushroom
31 Carried
32 Yawning gulf
34 "___ does it!"
35 Shoots in the jungle?
37 Kind of badge for a scout
38 Makes husky, as a voice
43 Martians and such
44 Sofa

45 Sailor's "yes!"
46 Poker stakes
47 "Comme ci, comme ça"
48 Chrysler, e.g.
49 "The Sun ___ Rises"
50 Trivial bit
51 New York footballers
52 Black-and-white cookie
53 Congers
54 Plenty ticked

by Jerry E. Rosman

ACROSS

1 Menachem's 1978 co-Nobelist
6 "Get out!"
11 ___ de Triomphe
14 Hanging need
15 Card game authority Edmond
16 Dull card game
17 Actress who was married to Dudley Moore
19 Fuss
20 Puts on a computer hard drive
21 Jeweled headpieces
23 Set down
24 Old Hartford hockey team
25 Rouse
29 Singer Cara
30 Hoops player
31 Say confidently
32 "___ Boot"
35 California city by Joshua Tree National Park
39 Blue
40 Sport ___ (popular vehicles)
41 "The Waste Land" poet
42 Summits
44 Hand-dyes with wax
45 Pilgrims to Mecca
48 "Wait a ___!"
49 Acid neutralizer
50 Most sugary
55 Compete
56 Trusting act
58 Night before
59 Golden award
60 Arm bones
61 Court divider
62 Rudder's place
63 Suspicious

DOWN

1 Prefix with disestablishmentarianism
2 Adjective follower
3 Afflictions
4 Like some mgrs.
5 Warning on the Enterprise
6 In a demure manner
7 Cud chewers
8 Deli bread
9 Sane
10 Highway divider
11 Not spaced-out
12 What Fuzzbusters detect
13 Angry
18 Fed head Greenspan
22 McSorley's product
24 Songbirds
25 New Testament book
26 Trumpet sound
27 Getting on in years
28 Mattel doll
29 Harvard, Yale, Brown, etc.
31 Poker starters
32 Half of MCIV
33 Run ___ (go crazy)
34 Fast jets, for short
36 Most tasty
37 Tranquil
38 Hgt.
42 In the style of
43 Parts of string quartets
44 Complaint
45 Whiz
46 Martini garnish
47 ___ shooting
48 Like court testimony
50 Practice in the ring
51 A fisherman may bring one home
52 "___ kleine Nachtmusik"
53 Restaurant review symbol
54 Those people
57 Good service?

by Peter Gordon

62

ACROSS

1 It's just one of those things
5 "Aw, shucks" expressions
10 More
14 Jealous wife in Greek myth
15 Slackened
16 A portion
17 "The moan of doves in immemorial ___": Tennyson
18 Campbell of "Martin"
19 Winter Palace ruler
20 Ready to swoon
23 "Go on..."
24 Clan emblem
25 Straight start?
27 Orbital periods
29 Actor McKellen
31 Birth control device
32 C.P.R. administrator
34 It ends in Mecca
35 Brit. legislators
36 Good-looking
40 Insulation ingredient, for short
41 Cooperstown nickname
42 Wool source
43 Bolo, for one
44 Michael Jordan's alma mater, in brief
45 Have it ___
49 Place for rings
51 Gives the gate
55 Genetic letters
56 Seedy-looking
59 ___ fide
60 Baptism and bris
61 L.A. gang member
62 Need a bath badly
63 Awaited a dubbing
64 Surrealist Magritte
65 Charger, to a Cockney
66 Lowly ones
67 Took habitually

DOWN

1 Tao, literally
2 Curtis of hair care
3 Loser of 1588
4 What to do?
5 "I ___ kick..."
6 Grammy winner Bonnie
7 Joe Jackson's "___ Really Going Out With Him?"
8 Book after Ezra
9 Minn. neighbor
10 Fruity-smelling compound
11 Experience a delay
12 They attract rubberneckers
13 Musket attachment
21 "C'mon, I wanna try!"
22 Gentile
26 Some E.R. cases
28 ___ judicata
30 "Song of the South" song syllables
33 Unable to decide
34 Shaker ___, O.
36 Satanic sort
37 Colorless solvents
38 Addictive stuff
39 Japanese capital
40 School grp.
46 Strasbourg siblings
47 Like lots of shopping now
48 Sang like Satchmo
50 Not out
52 Complete
53 Cliff projection
54 They may come in batteries
57 Torah holders
58 L'eggs shade
59 Term of address in the 'hood

by M. Francis Vuolo

ACROSS

1 "It's us against ___"
5 Backtalk
9 Data disk
14 What an optimist always has
15 This, south of the border
16 Bakery enticement
17 The "U" in I.C.U.
18 Larger ___ life
19 Circus star with a whip
20 1966 Johnny Rivers hit
23 Doozy
24 Suffix with pay or play
25 Capt.'s superior
28 Rock band ___ Mode
31 Cinder
34 Yale of Yale University
36 "Just ___ thought!"
37 Chorus member
38 Hospital ward alternative
42 Pentagon inventory
43 "Tip-Toe Thru the Tulips With Me" instrument
44 Make up (for)
45 Mudhole
46 Israeli parliament
49 Gave supper
50 ___-Cat (winter vehicle)
51 Currier's companion
53 1998 Best Picture nominee
60 Attacks
61 Opposed to, in dialect
62 Annapolis inits.
63 Tour of duty
64 Oodles
65 ___ for oneself

66 Short-tempered
67 As a result
68 Lawyers' charges

DOWN

1 As a result
2 Sharpen, as on a whetstone
3 "Ben-Hur," e.g.
4 Geo model
5 Medium-sized sofa
6 Equivalent to B flat
7 Dateless
8 Levelheaded
9 Longhorns, e.g.
10 Pulitzer Prize category
11 Capital of Italia
12 Gathering clouds, for one

13 Ruin
21 Turn out to be
22 Like a rare baseball game
25 Monument Valley features
26 On the ball
27 Force open, as a lock
29 Place for icicles
30 Civil War side: Abbr.
31 Standoffish
32 Slingshot ammo
33 ___ in on (neared)
35 Towel stitching
37 College major
39 Kind of sentence
40 Mamie's man
41 Moth-___
46 Hard to saw, as some pine

47 What a stucco house doesn't need
48 Be that as it may
50 Meager
52 Cram
53 After curfew
54 Sale caution
55 Doom
56 Composer Stravinsky
57 "Now it's clear"
58 Shakespeare's ___ Hathaway
59 Boys
60 Monogram of 40-Down's predecessor

by Gregory E. Paul

64

ACROSS

1 Farmland unit
5 News source of old
10 Summer getaway
14 Parade spoiler, perhaps
15 Ready to come off
16 Coloratura's piece
17 Back to being friends again?
19 Seasoned sailor
20 Ran into
21 They're sometimes fine
22 Choctaw and Chickasaw
24 St. Francis' birthplace
26 Actor James
27 Humor that doesn't cause a blush?
33 Do watercolors
36 "___ la vista"
37 Suffix with project
38 Big concert equipment
39 Skin suffixes
40 Worked-up state
41 Kelly's "___ Girls"
42 Mildew and such
43 Fountain drinks
44 Mentally sound?
47 One with an "Esq." tag
48 Zoo showoffs
52 Certain fir
55 Peak in Thessaly
57 Author Rita ___ Brown
58 Hullabaloos
59 Relapsing?
62 ___-majesté
63 Norman Vincent ___
64 More than suggest
65 Lascivious look
66 Mexicali mister
67 Batik artisan

DOWN

1 Sachet quality
2 Champs Élysées sights
3 Breaks in relations
4 Suffix with exist
5 Pastor
6 Dig like a pig
7 Written promises
8 Attendance fig., often
9 Goes back to the top
10 Pit boss's place
11 Riyadh native
12 Track event not in the Olympics
13 Praises for pups
18 Word before "a prayer" or "a clue"
23 Big Indian
25 Charged particles
26 "Far out, man!"
28 Writer with an award named after him
29 Florida's Key ___
30 Warm-hearted
31 Essayist's alias
32 6-2, 5-7, 6-3, etc.
33 ___ Alto
34 Hymn sign-off
35 ___ facto
39 They chase "bunnies"
40 Arrange logically
42 Greek cheese
43 Stiff hairs
45 Sadat's predecessor
46 Like much Jewish food
49 Manicurist's tool
50 Singer's span
51 Passover feast
52 Bouncer?
53 "Zip-___-Doo-Dah"
54 Get checkmated
55 In the blink ___ eye
56 Normandy battle site
60 License's cost
61 Nasty campaigning

by John Greenman

ACROSS

1 Bogus
6 Greeting with a smile
11 S.A.T. takers
14 Chosen ones
15 "Cry, the Beloved Country" author
16 10th-anniversary gift
17 [Hint] Apple on the head
19 Self center
20 Comparison figure
21 Lowest deck on a ship
22 Swear
23 VCR button
25 Water measurement
27 It might keep a shepherd awake
30 Pollen producer
32 Old Ford
33 Symbol of freshness
35 Kind of key
38 Come out
40 Pitch
42 The "greatest blessing" and the "greatest plague": Euripides
43 Little belittlement
45 Vaudeville dancer's prop
46 Not born yesterday
48 String decoration
50 Hiker, in a way
52 Refuse
54 Tramp's partner
55 Walpurgis Night figure
57 ___ Jones of old radio comedy
61 "You ___ here"
62 [Hint] Apple off the head
64 Annual awards giver
65 High points of a trip to South America?
66 Quartet member
67 A ship, to crew members
68 It raises dough
69 G.I. wear

DOWN

1 Sinn ___
2 What's more
3 Cordelia's father
4 Seafood dish
5 Busy person's abbr.
6 Copyists
7 Wild
8 Football legend Graham
9 Hype
10 "Barbara ___" (1966 hit)
11 [Hint] Apple in the head
12 Demanding standard
13 Buffaloes
18 Fanny Farmer treat
22 Mr. T's group
24 Slowly and evenly
26 Base
27 Squandered
28 Sphere starter
29 [Hint] Apple? Went ahead!
31 Classification
34 Superlative suffix
36 Missouri River tribe
37 Card-carrying
39 Foul
41 Image site
44 Cuddles
47 Bearish
49 Scheduled
50 Shuts (up)
51 Solid ground
53 Midsection
56 "M*A*S*H" star
58 Dissolve
59 Chili pot
60 Plug away
62 Kind of station
63 AT&T rival

by Greg Staples

66

ACROSS

1 Subject of a People profile
6 Hubbub
9 Father
13 Tylenol alternative
14 Temple worshiper
15 Single unit
16 Big crop in Hawaii
18 Goaded
19 End of some e-mail addresses
20 Opulence
21 Starry
22 Fix
24 Miami's ___ Bay
26 Mediocre
28 Cash register part
29 1941 Orson Welles classic
33 ___ Mahal
36 Fruity coolers
37 Note before la
38 Prefix with -nautics
39 Face off in the ring
40 Making a fuss
44 Pat Boone's "___ That a Shame"
45 Worry
46 Late prize-winning San Francisco columnist
50 Reef materials
54 Lucky charm
55 Diamond Head locale
57 Step to the plate
58 San Francisco footballer, briefly
59 Popular painkiller
61 Woman's lip application
62 "Feliz ___ nuevo"
63 Door swinger
64 E-mailed
65 Bench with a back
66 Law's partner

DOWN

1 One checking out a place in planning a crime
2 Escape the clutches of
3 Starting advantage
4 One of the Gabor sisters
5 "Symphonie fantastique" composer
6 "Stronger than dirt" sloganeer
7 Star in Cygnus
8 Have debts
9 Yahoo! or Lycos, e.g.
10 Furious
11 Song of triumph
12 Flummox
15 Biceps or triceps
17 Unlucky charm
21 "Q ___ queen"
23 Sale sign
25 Like slanted type
27 Kind of inspection
29 Taxi
30 Wedding vow
31 Cowboy's moniker
32 Some ring outcomes, for short
33 4:00 affair
34 Mr. Onassis
35 Music's ___ Bon Jovi
38 Tennis whiz
40 Kitchen gizmos
41 Med. school course
42 Cheesy snack
43 The mustachioed brother
44 Most skilled
46 Puts up, as a painting
47 Novelist Zola
48 Talk nonstop
49 Nary a soul
51 In ___ (trapped)
52 Oscar-winning Jessica
53 Navigate
56 Confess
59 Get a little shuteye
60 Tire filler

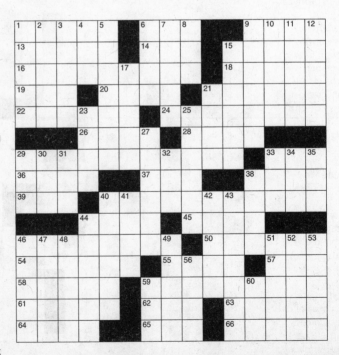

by David J. Kahn

ACROSS

1 Hula skirt material
6 Arafat's grp.
9 It may be secondhand
14 Moses' mountain
15 Varnish ingredient
16 Downy duck
17 Befuddle
18 Not cutting
20 Woman who's not very sharp?
22 Mad magazine's genre
25 Paint can direction
26 Addis Ababa's land: Abbr.
27 Mad. ___
29 Clip out
34 Chowed down
35 Stately shader
37 Every 9-Down has one
38 Girl who's got her facts wrong?
43 "Star Trek" extra
44 Cobbler
45 Windup
46 More spiteful
49 Chem. pollutant
51 Canonized Mlle.
52 New Mexico art center
54 The "N" in "N × P"
56 Man who's annually in the doghouse?
60 Aspirin target, maybe
61 Propelled a boat
65 The Little Mermaid
66 Coffee vessel
67 Extremist
68 Lavatory sign
69 Lipton product
70 Attack ad, maybe

DOWN

1 Govt. property org.
2 Purge
3 &
4 Pheasant ragout
5 ___ Nevada
6 Surveyor's map
7 Plasterwork backers
8 Fair-sized musical groups
9 Managua miss
10 Longish dress
11 Thor's father
12 Clark of the Daily Planet
13 Work unit
19 Cast-of-thousands film
21 Early evening
22 Chantey singer
23 Number one Hun
24 Grad student's work
28 Polar worker
30 Watch the kids
31 Most artful
32 Tooth: Prefix
33 Give, as an apology
36 Unruly locks
39 Harden
40 Hanky embroidery
41 Saw along the grain
42 City non-Muslims may not enter
47 Man addressed as "My Lord"
48 Cheap liquor
50 Louisiana waterways
53 English place name suffix
55 Poem of King David
56 Insignificant
57 Totally botch
58 Baseball's Saberhagen
59 Comedian Carvey
60 Henpeck
62 Rd. or hwy.
63 Unit of geologic time
64 Patriotic org.

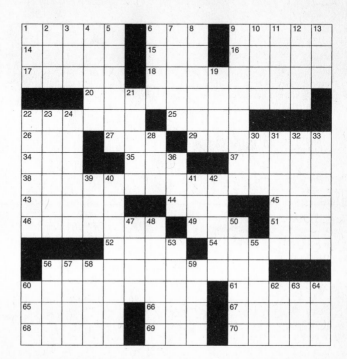

by Cynthia Joy Higgins

68

ACROSS

1 Nickname for 14-Down
7 His, in France
10 School of whales
13 Like a portion of some people's income
14 Plug, of a sort
15 It may be reached by tunnel
16 Cafeteria-goers
17 Hectorer of Zeus
18 Giant of old
19 Negative particle
20 Charlie's little sister
21 Game piece
22 Stethoscope user
23 ___'acte
25 Test pilot Chuck
27 In a sad way
29 School basics, in a way
30 "Wishing Will Make ___"
33 Chicken ___
34 Michael of R.E.M.
37 Anatomical holders
38 "Entry of Christ Into Brussels" artist
40 Tumbled
41 Bor-r-r-r-ring
43 Laborer of old
44 Subjects of a U.S. Air Force cover-up?
45 Messenger ___
46 Actress Claudia
48 Some trick-or-treaters
51 Command spot
52 Dance step
55 "Norma ___"
56 Boy with a blanket
58 Peanuts, in a manner of speaking
60 Furthermore
61 List ender
62 Not blatant
63 One who might be interested in big bucks
64 ___ bath (therapeutic treatment)
65 Ran on
66 What Marcie called 52-Down
67 ___-cone
68 Impatient agreement, maybe

DOWN

1 Place
2 32-Down's was a toy
3 Place for a chest
4 Stat start
5 Bit of truth?
6 QB's gains
7 Cartoonist Silverstein
8 At dawn
9 Marathon dancers, e.g.
10 Comment from Charlie Brown
11 Musical Shaw
12 Olympics length
14 This puzzle's honoree
20 Ms. magazine co-founder
24 Microwave
26 Dexterous
27 Ship officers
28 Actress De Carlo and others
30 Suffix akin to -esque
31 Chinese truth
32 Big Beethoven devotee
35 Mideast grp.
36 Chicago trains
39 It might give you a line
42 Like a bare floor
47 "Yeah, right!"
48 Alums
49 Capital west of Haiphong
50 Protest
52 Peppermint ___
53 Tree-lined walk
54 They're pulled uphill
57 Like some peacekeepers
59 New corp. hires
62 Plant, perhaps

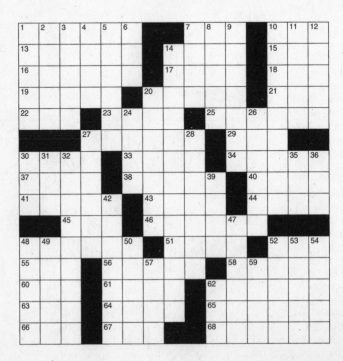

by Jim Page

ACROSS

1 Worker protection org.
5 Nuclear weapon
10 Cry from a crib
14 Smart-___
15 Rome's river
16 Eclipse, maybe, to the ancients
17 Shuttle launch sound
18 Verdi work
19 The African Queen, e.g.
20 1967 Van Morrison hit
23 Lose, as skin
24 "Erie Canal" mule
25 "___ la vista!"
28 The U.S.A.'s "uncle"
31 City west of Montgomery
35 Rooms with stairs leading to them
37 "Skip to My ___"
39 China's Chou En-___
40 Flowers given to the Preakness Stakes winner
44 Place with microscopes
45 14, in old Rome
46 Nail polish
47 Liability's opposite
50 Unused
52 Swap
53 Jabber
55 Reagan's first Secretary of State
57 1970 hit by Sugarloaf
63 Bring to 212 degrees
64 Charlie Chan portrayer Warner ___
65 Ooze
67 "Just this ___ ..."

68 Recoil in pain
69 Close tightly
70 Shade of red
71 In the buff
72 Grand Ole ___

DOWN

1 Dinghy propeller
2 One whose business isn't picking up?
3 Listen to
4 Word puzzle
5 United (with)
6 Humans, e.g.
7 Listen to
8 A ___ pittance
9 Slender nails
10 Ceiling-hung art
11 Love, Spanish-style
12 Lunch or dinner
13 Aardvark's tidbit
21 Hit with a bang

22 Car fill-up
25 "¿Usted ___ español?"
26 Map site
27 Knife wounds
29 Tylenol competitor
30 Up-to-date
32 Incan transport
33 Like a horse or lion
34 Bridal path
36 Reason for an X rating
38 Put to work
41 Yang's counterpart
42 Before
43 ___ Sea, in the North Atlantic
48 Hole for a lace
49 Menlo Park monogram
51 From what place?
54 On the map

56 Threw in
57 Auctioneer's last word
58 Paddy crop
59 Director Kazan
60 U.S. soldier in W.W. II
61 Not shallow
62 Four seasons
63 Go up and down in the water
66 Thickness

by Gregory E. Paul

ACROSS

1 Current units
5 Many comedy teams
9 Squirrel away
14 Some is junk
15 Archer of "Patriot Games"
16 Marseille menu
17 Collection in Old Icelandic
18 Carpe ___
19 "The ___ Incident" (1943 Fonda film)
20 Assume what's being asked
23 Parting word
24 Not happy
25 Flushed
27 Trinity member
28 Ginnie ___
30 Mystery writer Josephine
31 Mr. Potato Head part
32 Early Microsoft offering
33 "A mouse!"
34 Captures
35 Wake sleeping dogs, so to speak
39 ___ Jones's locker
40 NASDAQ listings: Abbr.
41 Speakers' pause fillers
42 Ending with methyl
43 Round Table title
44 Indy 500 logo
45 Place to take a cure
48 Cone bearer
49 Italian poet Torquato ___
51 Suffer a loss, slangily
53 Get closer to home, in a way
56 Not level
57 Like service station rags
58 Black-and-white hunter
59 ___ fatale
60 At liberty
61 Victory signs
62 Long lock
63 A.T.F. agents
64 To be, to Tiberius

DOWN

1 One-celled pond dwellers
2 Got by
3 Hardly the Queen's English
4 List of candidates
5 Miami-___ County
6 More than unusual
7 Get the better of
8 Academic term
9 Shipmate of Bones and Spock
10 Downtown cruiser
11 Like sloths and tree toads
12 Alley Oop's time
13 Chop down
21 Sitcom material
22 Search for
26 Welby and Kildare: Abbr.
29 Not gregarious
32 Like some martinis
33 Sci-fi visitors
34 Air rifle ammo
35 Item that may be slid down
36 Paycheck booster
37 Least fortunate
38 Called balls and strikes
39 Rock's ___ Leppard
43 The contiguous 48
44 Dirty
45 Oddballs may draw them
46 Zodiac fishes
47 "Ten-hut!" undoer
50 Talia of "Rocky"
52 Beyond's partner
54 "Desire Under the ___"
55 Cereal grasses
56 Toward the tiller

by Nick Grivas

ACROSS

1 It's in a jamb
5 Schoolmarmish
9 Outback Bowl city
14 To boot
15 NBC host
16 N.B.A. star called "The Shack"
17 Stout ingredient
18 Regarding
19 Hardly cutting-edge
20 Computer business?
22 Bit of color
23 Guitarist Paul
24 Sipping specialist
25 Rifle attachment
29 Show place
32 NATO members
34 Nature of cyberspace?
39 Wash out
40 Center
42 Suffix with buck
43 Combining on the Internet?
45 Risk
47 Synthetic fiber
49 Tetra- plus one
50 Say
54 Bolivian bear
56 Chili rating unit?
57 What makes people write LOL?
63 Christina Applegate sitcom
64 Litter's littlest
65 Name that rings a bell?
66 Writer Chekhov
67 Manger visitors
68 Sitar music
69 Doesn't possess
70 Gulf of ___, off the coast of Yemen
71 Feel sure about

DOWN

1 Woman of rank
2 Haakon's royal successor
3 2-Down's capital
4 Univ. marchers
5 Part of a service
6 Put up a fight
7 Division word
8 Phobos, to Mars
9 Mexicali munchie
10 Opposition
11 Had in mind
12 Satchel in Cooperstown
13 Birch relative
21 Sheltered, at sea
24 Kind of serum
25 Cracker's target
26 Symbol of happiness
27 Ye follower
28 Place for a shore dinner
30 Alternative to a fence
31 Binet data
33 Brat's look
35 Take it easy
36 Qum home
37 Reason for a suit
38 Skywalker's mentor
41 Roadside stop
44 Piece of clothing
46 Each
48 Lizard's locale?
50 Indian chief
51 "Maria ___" (old tune)
52 Brig's pair
53 Gasoline may make it go
55 Protest of a sort
57 Witty Bombeck
58 Campus area
59 Picnic spot
60 Russian Everyman
61 Canceled, to NASA
62 Nibble away

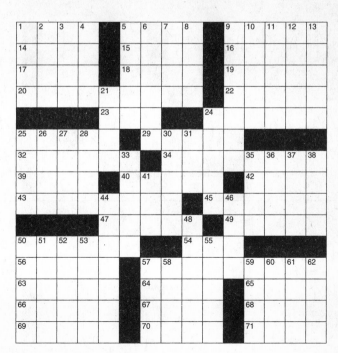

by Richard Silvestri

ACROSS

1 Linemen's protectors
5 Light-refracting crystal
10 Marries
14 Coward in "The Wizard of Oz"
15 Author Bret
16 Like slanted type: Abbr.
17 The New Yorker cartoonist Peter
18 ___ a time (individually)
19 Kind of wrestling
20 Buddhist discipline
21 Soul singer from California?
23 Slowly, to a conductor
25 Bullfight bull
26 California prison
29 Big airplane engine
33 Lustrous gems
35 Levi's material
37 Coronado's gold
38 Prayer opener
39 Kind of boom
40 Fake
41 Greyhound, e.g.
42 Heard, but not seen
43 Intelligence
44 Old-time Japanese governor
46 Tried and true
48 "What are the ___?"
50 St. Petersburg's Hermitage, e.g.
53 Pop singer from Texas?
58 Wizards and Magic org.
59 Grad
60 Mt. Everest locale
61 "___ calling"
62 Italian money
63 Jalopy
64 Darjeeling and oolong
65 Hit the runway
66 Snake shapes
67 Johnson of "Laugh-In"

DOWN

1 Public square
2 On TV
3 Country singer from North Dakota?
4 ___-Cat (off-road vehicle)
5 Snaps
6 Indian princess
7 Infuriates
8 Get the ball rolling
9 Momentarily dazzling
10 Opposite of ignorance
11 Sewing case
12 Cousin of "Phooey!"
13 Wade (through)
21 Works at the Louvre
22 Short drink
24 Olympian's quest
27 Nose tickler
28 ___ Work (road repair sign)
30 Folk-rock singer from Colorado?
31 Great times
32 Scholarly book
33 Cutlass or Eighty Eight
34 "Tush!"
36 Christie's "Death on the ___"
39 Big film festival name
40 Envisages
42 Autobahn car
43 Flabbergast
45 Became angry
47 Beams
49 Litigants
51 German sub
52 Parsonage
53 ___ Mall (London street)
54 Inter ___
55 Become a traitor
56 They'll get you in hot water
57 Noted gallery
61 ___ loss for words

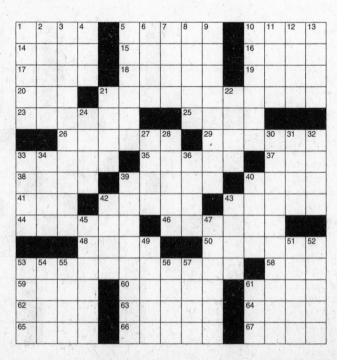

by Dave and Diane Epperson

ACROSS
1 Atty.-to-be's exam
5 Edith who sang "La Vie en Rose"
9 Key of Mozart's Symphony No. 39
14 Court records
15 Stewpot
16 Said à la the Raven
17 Feature of some shirts
19 "I give!"
20 "Seinfeld" miss
21 Bite, as the heels
23 Crisscross pattern
25 Catch in the act
26 Big goon
29 Decade divs.
30 "Minnie the Moocher" singer
33 See 13-Down
34 "Gil Blas" writer
35 Neuter
38 "Not ___ bet!"
40 Alkaline solutions
41 Help run, as a party
44 Part of WASP
47 Qatar, for one
49 Cone bearer
52 Fighter in gray
53 Biddy
54 Fish in a can
56 Part of a TV feed
58 "The Devil's Dictionary" author
59 In any respect
62 Baltimore chef's specialty
64 Kindled anew
65 Roof projection
66 Get out of bed
67 Intense media campaign
68 Amscrayed
69 Tolkien tree creatures

DOWN
1 In recent days
2 Like some variables
3 Times up
4 Unspoken
5 Malodorous animal
6 Needing hospital care
7 Astronaut Shepard
8 Hot breakfast dish
9 Steady
10 "Candid Camera" man
11 ___ cit. (footnote abbr.)
12 U.S./U.K. divider
13 With 33-Across, Montreal's subway
18 In a state of abeyance
22 Heavy sheet
24 River of Aragón
26 On vacation
27 Web designer's creation
28 Baby blues
31 Sir Arthur ___ Doyle
32 Capital on a fjord
33 "Butt out!," initially
35 Surgery result
36 Dermal opening
37 Ishmael's captain
39 Tiny colonists
42 Klink's aide in "Hogan's Heroes"
43 Two-___ sloth
45 Got one's mitts on
46 Ira Gershwin's contribution
48 Social welfare org.
49 Quarter-barrel
50 Theme of "Oedipus Rex"
51 ___ Pieces
55 "The Wreck of the Mary ___"
56 Touched down
57 Like some vaccines
59 Wall St. whiz
60 Bus. card abbr.
61 ___ Baba
63 Caesar's hello

by Fred Piscop

ACROSS

1 Fusses
5 Clairvoyant's claim
8 Functioning
14 OUTFIELDER
15 Chowed down
16 Projectionist's target
17 SECOND BASEMAN
19 Did a bootblack's job
20 Jotting down
22 Start of the 18th century
23 Baseball stat
26 "Wait a ___!"
27 "___ tu" (Verdi aria)
29 Donna Shalala's dept.
30 Arafat of the P.L.O.
32 Courtroom V.I.P.
34 With 42-Across, what the 10 answers to the capitalized clues comprise
38 Literary adverb
39 Mr. Onassis, familiarly
40 Harem rooms
42 See 34-Across
47 Posts
48 Priced to move
49 Draft org.
52 As well
53 United Nations Day mo.
54 Acid
55 What the fat lady sings?
57 SHORTSTOP
60 "___ ergo sum"
62 OUTFIELDER
66 LEFT-HANDED PITCHER
67 Actress Sue ___ Langdon

68 OUTFIELDER
69 Like some inclement weather
70 Go down
71 Opportunity

DOWN

1 Airport abbr.
2 Twosome
3 Handicapper's place: Abbr.
4 Tibia
5 New York's time zone
6 Zeno, for one
7 Ivy League school, briefly
8 ___ Enterprise
9 THIRD BASEMAN
10 Parched
11 CATCHER
12 Moocher

13 "The ___ near!"
18 ___-um (gnat)
21 FIRST BASEMAN
23 RIGHT-HANDED PITCHER
24 Cotton bundles
25 ___ of Langerhans
28 King, in Cádiz
31 Beat it
32 Goes bad
33 Almost an eternity
35 One who hems, but doesn't haw
36 "Let's Make ___"
37 Heavy hammers
41 Went like a leadfoot
43 Knocking sound
44 Spanish uncle
45 Small curl of hair
46 Pentium processor maker

49 Punches
50 Wind up
51 Musical transition
53 Put one's two cents in
56 Abundant
58 "___ a Teen-age Werewolf"
59 Steals, old-style
61 ___-10 (acne-fighting medicine)
63 Sound of delight
64 Muscle: Prefix
65 Fast wings

by Peter Gordon

ACROSS

1 Nurse's item
5 Some change
10 "The Far Pavilions" author M. M. ___
14 Worrying words from a driver
15 Campaign stop, e.g.
16 "Shoo!"
17 St. Bernard sound
18 "Cheers" barmaid
19 Little dog, for short
20 1936 film starring 57-Across
23 Row
24 1934 film starring 57-Across
28 Compass line
31 Treated with contempt
34 Fam. member
35 1938 film starring 57-Across
37 Actress Dee
39 Target of some creams
40 Lakers' org.
42 Road shoulder
43 Many winter vacationers
46 1949 film starring 57-Across
49 Abbr. on a business letter
50 Tchotchke holder
52 NNW's opposite
53 1957 film starring 57-Across
55 Bub
57 Actor born April 5, 1900
63 Shake up
66 Ernest ___, winner of the first Pulitzer for fiction
67 Greek liqueur
68 Zone
69 Gallops
70 Stick in one's ___
71 Tough test, informally
72 Pass
73 Marx with a manifesto

DOWN

1 Farm females
2 Rider's command
3 In a few minutes
4 Like some shows
5 Actress Yvonne
6 "Terrible" one
7 Ford product, briefly
8 Sign up
9 Socks away
10 "Wham!"
11 Knock over
12 Gab
13 Electric ___
21 Air-filled item, maybe
22 Last part
25 Info for waiters
26 Kind of wheel
27 How some steak is served
28 Humiliated
29 "All-American" fellow
30 Hardly optimists
32 Have
33 Remove from a sack
36 "Understand?"
38 Measurements overseer: Abbr.
41 Drink suffix
44 Legal defendant: Abbr.
45 Church part
47 Chair part
48 Gist
51 When there's darkness, in a Koestler title
54 Relatively cool sun
56 Butter holder
58 Club of song
59 Utility abbr.
60 Emanation
61 6-Down, e.g.
62 Long, dismal cry
63 Quick punch
64 Vein pursuit
65 Flock's place

by Frances Hansen

The New York Times

CROSSWORDS

SMART PUZZLES PRESENTED WITH STYLE

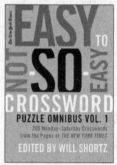

Available at your local bookstore or online at nytimes.com/nytstore.

 St. Martin's Griffin

1

```
ABLE . LATHE . CRAM
RAIN . ACRES . LANE
ABCDAYTIMEHOSTS
BEE . NMEX . OSHEA
. MIA . MARE .
FILMNOMINATION
LADLE . DOLES . LBO
ERLE . GETIT . VOID
AGE . DONEE . ZESTS
FORMERSTUDENTS
ALEE . OLD
BEAST . BAND . SHA
ALPHABETQUARTET
ELEE . ALEUT . EURO
REDS . TINAS . ADAM
```

2

```
FRAGS . ALA . EDGE
RENOIR . BAREBEAR
ALGORE . OPENBARS
MOOSEMOUSSE . RET
EARED . NNE . SAD
DDAY . LADDS . REBA
. POI . ESTEEM
GOB . ORR . PIE . REA
ERODED . ANT
MEAD . SACRE . CPAS
. RES . DOE . SLAIN
ORB . HOARSEHORSE
COOLIDGE . RESALE
HAREHAIR . NEEDER
OMEN . YOS . PRESS
```

3

```
RAJAH . BRIM . OATS
ALONE . AURA . USES
ITSTRIKESMETHAT
NOSE . DER . ALTERS
. NOOR . ABBA .
FRANKLYSPEAKING
LAMAS . USA . EVIL
UZI . PAGER . AKA
FOGS . UPA . PINON
FROMWHEREISTAND
. AILS . ISIS .
COARSE . ALL . ACME
ASITHASBEENSAID
FADE . SALE . RISKY
EYED . EDEN . ANTES
```

4

```
PRADO . FRAY . AMFM
SUNUP . ROPE . SALE
ISNTTHATSPECIAL
STAY . OGEE . WONK
. CBER . METS .
EBAY . ASHES . TEE
SPELT . NOON . ARMY
WELLEXCUUUSEME
EELS . MERS . SPAYS
EST . PASSE . ELMS
. HMOS . OKRA .
TEEN . HARE . NCAA
NICEGOINGGENIUS
BEAT . FLEA . GENTS
ARTS . TOWN . ODEON
```

5

```
LASSO . ODDS . BAIT
AUTOS . RARE . ANNO
WRATH . BRIM . CAAN
NAG . KNITPICKING
. POET . NAUSEA
OGRESS . LSATS .
KNIGHTCOURT . LET
RAMS . LTR . AERO
AWE . KNOTFORSALE
. ELOPE . DECKED
OUTRUN . SETH .
KNEWMOWNHAY . AGO
ACTI . INCA . PAVED
YARN . LBAR . ECOLI
SPAS . YARD . SENSE
```

6

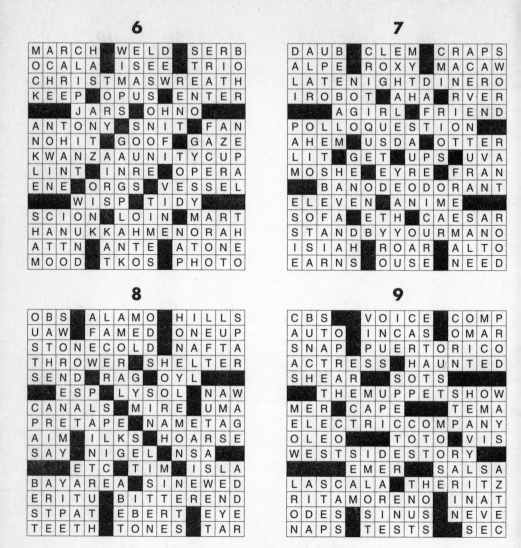

M	A	R	C	H	■	W	E	L	D	■	S	E	R	B
O	C	A	L	A	■	I	S	E	E	■	T	R	I	O
C	H	R	I	S	T	M	A	S	W	R	E	A	T	H
K	E	E	P	■	O	P	U	S	■	E	N	T	E	R
■	■	■	J	A	R	S	■	O	H	N	O	■	■	■
A	N	T	O	N	Y	■	S	N	I	T	■	F	A	N
N	O	H	I	T	■	G	O	O	F	■	G	A	Z	E
K	W	A	N	Z	A	A	U	N	I	T	Y	C	U	P
L	I	N	T	■	I	N	R	E	■	O	P	E	R	A
E	N	E	■	O	R	G	S	■	V	E	S	S	E	L
■	■	W	I	S	P	■	T	I	D	Y	■	■	■	■
S	C	I	O	N	■	L	O	I	N	■	M	A	R	T
H	A	N	U	K	K	A	H	M	E	N	O	R	A	H
A	T	T	N	■	A	N	T	E	■	A	T	O	N	E
M	O	O	D	■	T	K	O	S	■	P	H	O	T	O

7

D	A	U	B	■	C	L	E	M	■	C	R	A	P	S
A	L	P	E	■	R	O	X	Y	■	M	A	C	A	W
L	A	T	E	N	I	G	H	T	D	I	N	E	R	O
I	R	O	B	O	T	■	A	H	A	■	R	V	E	R
■	■	■	A	G	I	R	L	■	F	R	I	E	N	D
P	O	L	L	O	Q	U	E	S	T	I	O	N	■	■
A	H	E	M	■	U	S	D	A	■	O	T	T	E	R
L	I	T	■	G	E	T	■	U	P	S	■	U	V	A
M	O	S	H	E	■	E	Y	R	E	■	F	R	A	N
■	■	B	A	N	O	D	E	O	D	O	R	A	N	T
E	L	E	V	E	N	■	A	N	I	M	E	■	■	■
S	O	F	A	■	E	T	H	■	C	A	E	S	A	R
S	T	A	N	D	B	Y	Y	O	U	R	M	A	N	O
I	S	I	A	H	■	R	O	A	R	■	A	L	T	O
E	A	R	N	S	■	O	U	S	E	■	N	E	E	D

8

O	B	S	■	A	L	A	M	O	■	H	I	L	L	S
U	A	W	■	F	A	M	E	D	■	O	N	E	U	P
S	T	O	N	E	C	O	L	D	■	N	A	F	T	A
T	H	R	O	W	E	R	■	S	H	E	L	T	E	R
S	E	N	D	■	R	A	G	■	O	Y	L	■	■	■
■	■	E	S	P	■	L	Y	S	O	L	■	N	A	W
C	A	N	A	L	S	■	M	I	R	E	■	U	M	A
P	R	E	T	A	P	E	■	N	A	M	E	T	A	G
A	I	M	■	I	L	K	S	■	H	O	A	R	S	E
S	A	Y	■	N	I	G	E	L	■	N	S	A	■	■
■	■	E	T	C	■	T	I	M	■	I	S	L	A	■
B	A	Y	A	R	E	A	■	S	I	N	E	W	E	D
E	R	I	T	U	■	B	I	T	T	E	R	E	N	D
S	T	P	A	T	■	E	B	E	R	T	■	E	Y	E
T	E	E	T	H	■	T	O	N	E	S	■	T	A	R

9

C	B	S	■	V	O	I	C	E	■	C	O	M	P	■
A	U	T	O	■	I	N	C	A	S	■	O	M	A	R
S	N	A	P	■	P	U	E	R	T	O	R	I	C	O
A	C	T	R	E	S	S	■	H	A	U	N	T	E	D
■	■	■	T	H	E	M	U	P	P	E	T	S	H	O	W
M	E	R	■	C	A	P	E	■	■	T	E	M	A	■
E	L	E	C	T	R	I	C	C	O	M	P	A	N	Y
O	L	E	O	■	■	T	O	T	O	■	V	I	S	■
W	E	S	T	S	I	D	E	S	T	O	R	Y	■	■
■	■	■	E	M	E	R	■	■	S	A	L	S	A	■
L	A	S	C	A	L	A	■	T	H	E	R	I	T	Z
R	I	T	A	M	O	R	E	N	O	■	I	N	A	T
O	D	E	S	■	S	I	N	U	S	■	N	E	V	E
N	A	P	S	■	T	E	S	T	S	■	S	E	C	■

10

I	N	C	A	S	H	■	T	O	V	■	W	H	O	S
P	E	O	R	I	A	■	E	R	I	■	H	U	R	T
O	U	T	E	R	R	A	N	K	S	■	I	B	L	E
D	R	Y	■	P	V	T	■	C	A	R	B	O	N	■
■	■	K	N	I	G	H	T	E	R	R	A	N	T	■
A	D	I	E	U	S	■	I	R	I	S	H	■	■	■
G	A	N	G	S	T	E	R	R	A	P	■	U	L	M
A	N	T	S	■	S	U	E	■	■	A	B	A	A	■
R	A	E	■	P	E	T	E	R	R	A	B	B	I	T
■	R	A	I	S	E	■	O	N	E	A	C	T	■	■
C	O	M	M	U	T	E	R	R	A	I	L	■	■	■
U	N	E	A	S	E	■	A	I	D	■	H	O	W	■
R	A	Z	Z	■	L	A	N	D	B	R	I	D	G	E
S	I	Z	E	■	L	S	U	■	E	A	S	T	L	A
E	R	O	S	■	E	S	P	■	D	O	O	V	E	R

```
L I L L I   M I I I   M A Z E
U N I O N   I N C A   I D E A
R F K S T A D I U M   T E A R
E R E   O M I T   B A G E L S
D A S H T O   I C I E R
    M O R T A R   S A N T A
T A B S   E R L E   O D I U M
O N E P M   O R T   P U L S E
R A D I I   M E A T   A S K S
A G E N T   P A N O U T
    A Z T E C   P N E U M O
R A F F I A   T O I L   L E G
A R L O   M R I S C A N N E R
S T I R   P O O H   C E A S E
H Y P E   A N N A   E A S E S
```

```
S T U D   G E N A   A G N E W
H Y P O   O L A V   L E A S H
O P E N   S O M E   B E T S Y
P E N E L O P E C R U Z
S A N T A F E   E M E R I L
    H U T   T I L   R O T O
I D T A G   M O T I F   S S R
S O U T H S E A S C R U I S E
L O G   S H A D Y   O N E O N
A N A T   A N Y   O L D
M E T E O R   T R I E S T E
  C L E A N U P C R E W S
M O T H S   R O S H   A L I T
A N N I E   A N K A   G E N E
E A T E N   B O S N   E S S E
```

```
F R O G   S A B O T   P O P S
R I M A   A G O R A   O R E L
O N O R   T O T A L   T I R E
  G O B L I N O N E S F O O D
    O N Y X   P U N T S
E L S I E   U R A L
S A N D W I T C H E S   D U B
S H O O   G U I O N   P E R O
O R B   H O T G H O U L A S H
    P E R U   P O L A R
P E A L E   A S I T
E L F E L F A S P R O U T S
R A T A   I N T R O   R O A D
E T E S   S K E I N   D R N O
S E R E   C A R T S   U N D O
```

```
W H O A   M O S A I C   U L E
H I N T   O P E N T O   H A T
I T E M   B A L D E R D A S H
G A S   K I L L S   S O U S A
  S E O U L   R E V L O N
B L A T H E R S K I T E
O U T I N   E P I C S   T I P
A M E S   R H I N O   C O N E
S P R   D E A L T   L A N C E
  G O B B L E D Y G O O K
E R R A T A   O N E A M
L O O S E   P E A C E   V E G
F L A P D O O D L E   M A T E
I F S   O R E G O N   G I A N
N E T   N O T Y E T   M L X X
```

```
T A T A   O N U S   P R A D O
O B I T   F E S T   R E S I N
M E E T S F A C E T O F A C E
S T R I P     G R A F   P E A
  L A N E   E M I L
  S T A N D S T O E T O T O E
A L I   K A T E   S N A R L
L E A N   K E E P S   G R A M
P E R O N   N E A L   D T S
S T A R E S E Y E T O E Y E
  A M I N   R E G S
A B E   E G G S   A C H O O
W A L K S H A N D I N H A N D
A D L A I   G O O D   E L I E
Y E A T S   E W E S   W E T S
```

16

S	C	A	L	P		A	M	I	S		A	D	A	M
T	A	L	E	S		P	A	S	T		S	A	G	O
A	L	L	A	H		O	S	L	O		L	R	O	N
M	I	C	H	A	E	L	K	E	A	T	O	N		
E	P	A		W	A	L	E		S	U	P	E	R	B
N	E	S	S		S	O	D	A		F	E	R	I	A
	R	H	E	T	T		F	I	A	T		S	O	T
		V	A	L	K	I	L	M	E	R				
M	I	R		T	A	I	L		O	D	E	L	L	
A	D	A	P	T		A	M	E	R		M	E	O	W
N	I	N	E	O	F		H	O	A	X		O	R	R
	G	E	O	R	G	E	C	L	O	O	N	E	Y	
J	E	E	R		Y	O	R	E		U	T	I	L	E
A	T	R	A		E	T	O	N		T	O	N	E	S
W	E	S	T		R	O	S	E		S	E	E	I	T

17

K	E	E	L		R	A	M	P	S		A	F	A	R
N	Y	S	E		I	D	E	A	L		B	O	L	O
O	R	S	O	N	B	E	A	N	O		O	N	T	O
T	E	E	N	I	E	S	T			M	U	Z	A	K
			I	C	Y			A	T	I	T			
N	O	P		K	E	N	O	G	R	I	F	F	E	Y
A	M	A	S	S		O	R	E	O		A	L	E	E
B	A	L	I		S	T	O	N	Y		C	O	R	A
O	N	I	N		P	A	N	T		L	E	W	I	S
B	I	N	G	O	C	R	O	S	B	Y		N	E	T
		A	D	A	Y			A	S	K				
G	R	A	P	E			E	S	T	O	N	I	A	N
O	U	Z	O		T	R	E	N	T	L	O	T	T	O
O	D	O	R		A	U	R	A	L		W	C	T	U
N	E	V	E		G	R	O	P	E		S	H	U	N

18

O	N	R	Y	E		S	A	R	A	N		D	A	B
B	A	C	O	N		E	L	O	P	E		I	G	O
S	H	A	K	E	S	P	E	A	R	E		L	A	W
		E	M	O	T	E	D		S	M	A	Z	E	
D	U	B	L	I	N		S	C	O	O	P	E	R	
O	S	U		E	Y	E	S		A	N	N	I		
G	U	L	F	S		A	T	M	S		I	D	E	A
M	A	L	L		F	R	U	I	T		C	A	R	T
A	L	F	A		O	L	D	S		N	A	T	A	L
	I	N	C	A		Y	O	G	A		E	S	A	
B	I	G	G	A	M	E		A	S	I	D	E	S	
O	T	H	E	R		V	A	U	L	T	S			
R	A	T		H	A	I	R	R	A	I	S	I	N	G
O	L	E		O	R	L	O	N		E	U	R	O	S
N	O	R		P	E	S	O	S		R	E	A	T	A

19

P	A	D	S		A	S	S	A	M		T	H	D	
E	L	E	C		N	I	T	R	O		R	E	I	N
A	L	F	A		T	R	U	E	R		O	H	N	O
C	H	I	L	L	I	E	R	W	E	A	T	H	E	R
H	E	A	D	Y		M	E	N	U		E	D	U	
E	R	N		S	I	E		O	R	P	H	A	N	
S	E	T	S		A	N	E	S		A	S	S	T	S
		W	I	L	D	G	E	E	S	E				
S	C	R	A	M		S	G	T	S		C	A	D	S
C	H	U	M	P	S		H	S	T		N	A	H	
O	I	D		E	A	S	E		W	A	C	K	Y	
F	L	O	R	I	D	A	V	A	C	A	T	I	O	N
F	I	L	A		D	R	I	V	E		T	E	T	E
S	E	P	T		L	A	C	E	D		I	N	A	S
	S	H	E		E	N	T	R	E		C	T	N	S

20

A	M	A	H	S		S	C	A	P	E		A	B	A
L	O	G	A	N		E	L	I	A	S		N	O	W
A	T	R	I	A		R	U	N	T	S		D	N	A
S	H	A	R	K	T	E	E	T	H		E	R	I	K
		N	E	O	N			E	F	F	E	T	E	
S	L	U	E		W	A	Y	S	T	A	T	I	O	N
S	O	F	T	G		E	P	I	C	S				
T	O	O		R	E	E	N	A	C	T		A	M	I
		F	A	U	S	T			S	E	V	E	N	
H	O	P	E	F	L	O	A	T	S		Y	A	N	K
U	S	E	D	T	O		E	A	S	E				
B	I	T	S		G	R	E	A	T	W	H	I	T	E
C	R	U		R	I	O	T	S		I	O	N	I	C
A	I	L		O	Z	O	N	E		G	L	I	N	T
P	S	A		B	E	T	A	S		S	E	T	T	O

21

```
D I S C   S M A S H   A S P S
U T A H   E S T E E   S P A M
C O M E O N D O W N   S I N E
    A M O O N   P L U N G E
B U T T E R S   C A I R O
A T H E N S   B A R T E R E D
D O E R     N O R T H   S S E
E P A   G O O D B Y E   O P S
G I N   O B O E S   A L I A
G A S M A S K S   M A R V E L
    W I P E S   F O R R E S T
C R E M E S   E A T M E
H E R O   S U R V E Y S A Y S
I B I S   E A S E L   T R A Y
N A S A   D R E S S   S K Y S
```

22

```
L E G S   H I T I T   B A S S
A L O T   A N I S E   A R C O
H O W A R D K E E L   Y E A R
R I N G O   D E L A W A R E
        G A Z A     A B A
A C E   D A N I E L S T E R N
D U N   S P I R A L   C L U E
H O S T   M I T   H U N T
O M O O   P A S S E S   D O W
C O R D E L L H U L L   E N T
      I R A   P I A F
G R E E N T E A   S L E E T
L O A F   O R R I N H A T C H
I M S O   O G I V E   P A R E
B E E R   N O D E D   S T U N
```

23

```
B L A B S   F A R E D   A B C
A U D I T   I M B R O G L I O
S N I D E   L O I N C L O T H
I C E   A C L U   S O T T O
C H U C K B E R R Y   B A Y S
      U S S   E A S E L
R O I L   A I S L E   I Z E
R U M P E L S T I L T S K I N
S T P   L E T O N   W E P T
      R E F E R   A L A
A T O N   R O U N D A B O U T
L O V E S   T O O T   G N U
P R I M E C U T S   H E L I X
E A S Y T O S E E   A R E T E
S H E   H E A R D   M A R E S
```

24

```
S W E P T   A J A R   S I P S
P A T I O   N O P E   T N U T
A D A G E   E K E D   R A R A
      S H O W E R S H O W E R
S K I T O W     A V E R T
M O B I L E M O B I L E
E A S E D   I M O F F   C P R
A L E S   P A N T S   S H O O
R A N   C O M I C   C O A S T
      P O L I S H P O L I S H
C L E A N   E N U R E S
A U G U S T A U G U S T
R A Y S   E X P O   O I L E D
D U P E   A L T O   L O T T O
S S T S   L E O N   E N R O N
```

25

```
F I R S T   A L G A   B L I P
A C T O R   L O O N   R I T A
T H E M E   S A L T   A L A S
      B A D O F F I C I A L S
S C A R C E       U N C L E
A R E E L E C T E D B Y
B A R R Y   H O N E S   N I P
E Z I O   M A N L Y   N A N A
R Y E   D O R I A   M E D A L
      G O O D C I T I Z E N S
S C R O D       O S P R E Y
W H O D O N O T V O T E
A I D S   A L O E   O R T H O
I D E O   S I D E   O C E A N
N E O N   H O O P   K E N Y A
```

26

```
E S P . . J I G S . A N W A R
O L E G . A G R A . N O R M A
N A N A . G O O K . A T E A T
. W A L P U R G I S N A C H T
. . L E A . . T I N K L Y . .
S T G E O R G E S D A Y . . .
P E R O N . H R O S S . M M E
E R I N . A R R . K I E V .
W I N . C A N O E . T E N S E
. . S O L A R N E W Y E A R .
I S T H M I . . D I E . . . .
P A N A M E R I C A N D A Y .
A T O N E . A D A M . U L A N
S A T I N . J O K E . P I L E
S N E A D . A L E S . T E D .
```

27

```
F A I R . B A L D . B O Y E R
U L N A . R H E A . E N E R O
R E D B R E A S T . T A L I A
. . B U Y . E E G S . L T S
A S P I R E S . D R O P O U T
S T U . A R A B . A N E W .
C O R A L . F L A N . E B A N
A M P S . B E A R D . V E N I
P A L O . A R C O . T E L E X
. E N I D . K O B E . L Y E
S C H E M E R . M O N E Y E D
C O E . P N E U . L O B .
O M A H A . G R E E N B A C K
P E R I L . A G A R . E X P O
E S T E E . L E T O . D E U S
```

28

```
S C O W . I L S A . C H I T S
A R L O . L O A D . R I C H E
W E E W I L L I E W I N K I E
N E G . G I L D . A T T E N D
. . W A N E . A R I . S K Y
V E N I V I D I V I C I . .
E X I L E . . D O N . N Y E T
T A L L . T H I N G . F O T O
S M E E . O O O . M A G O O
. . M A K E M I N E M I N K
W E D . L I S . G O R Y .
A N I M A L . I N R E . B U S
L O V E S L A B O R S L O S T
S L E E K . P E R I . I D E A
H A S T A . E X E S . D E R N
```

29

```
A V E R . B R E D . A D A M
C O R E . L I E U . S C O N E
T W I C E T O L D . E Q U A L
A S C O T . . S C R U B .
. . R A T I O . A V I L A
. O D D L O T S . B I R E M E
D A I S . R A T S . L E T O N
E X T . V I L L A G E . A L Y
P A T T I . Y E L L . F L E A
S C O R N S . R E E B O K S
. A M A T I . S M E A R .
. A N N E S . . J A U N T
F O R C E . T W O B A G G E R
I N K E R . U R D U . E L L E
B O S S . B Y E S . S I L K
```

30

```
B O D E . A T O P . T E R S E
I N O N . R O M A . K N E A D
A C L O C K W O R K O R A N G
S E T U P . T O R E . O R G Y
. . G A R R . O P E L . .
S A S H . B U S T I N L O O S
O R E . P I C T . S E E F I T
D O D G E . K E R . M E A L Y
O M E L E T . R O R Y . G E L
M A R A T H O N M A . M E D E
. . S E A N . A J A R . .
W O E S . W E A N . E B O L I
A N D J U S T I C E F O R A L
S O N A R . W R E N . N E I L
P R A W N . O S S O . D O R Y
```

31

```
PAPA  LEASH   ISNT
ILLS  ALBEE   STIR
CLASSCLOWN   LUNA
TENET  AMEN   ADAM
SNORED  BRAWNY
     TROT   ADHOC
LADS  NOSHER  ADO
ICE  ANATOMY  LIT
ALA  NATURE   KLEE
RUNON    ANDA
   SCARFS  DERAIL
LOLA   IOUS  LASSO
AVIS  GYMTEACHER
LESE  OLMOS   HERR
ARTY  REAPS   ISEE
```

32

```
ABET  TAMPA   OLLA
LAVA  EMILY   NEAR
TRIX  NOLAN   BATE
ONLIBERTY   ORRIN
     ETA  MADONNA
SPOON  LUANDA
HORNET  STA   DRAB
ALLY  ETHER   WILE
YOYO  MAE   MEANIE
    UMPIRE  TYKES
QUARREL    STU
UNITS  ONTHINICE
ITSO  BRAHE   ONLY
TILE  RENES   STAR
OLES  ADORE   HOPE
```

33

```
IANS  BATOR   ACHE
OMIT  ADAGE   SUIT
WATERWORLD   WREN
ASTRAL  PEA   ITSA
 SINKER   SCARF
   LEDON  TILLED
COPY   TUMOR   ODE
UPI  ADORERS   ONE
RAP  FIRST   ADAM
BLEARS   EARLS
  BLOTS  LEAKEY
BOOM  AAH  STARED
ELMO  FLUSHINGNY
ALBS  FOLIO   COTE
MAST  SNARE   ETAS
```

34

```
HASH  BLOT   SHREW
AGHA  LOAN   TOOTH
PRINCEOFTHECITY
PERSIANS   ANKLES
YET  CRY   TWOS
   PAY  BEAS   CAB
STEED  ALAI   SOSO
ASTRANGERINTOWN
LANK  EENY   OAKEN
ERA  SEND   BRR
   SODA  RAM   LAS
POSTAL  CIAAGENT
ITTAKESAVILLAGE
STOLE  OPEN   ISLE
HOPED  BERG   BEEP
```

35

```
  SEM  DISC  EARNS
GERE  ISLE   UBOAT
AURA  MEAD   GETTY
FRANKIEVALET
FANTAN   RAN   UGH
ETD  PICT  DEBBIE
    PUSHES   RELY
  MARTHASTEWARD
SALE   STATIC
PIMPLE  ABCS   SRI
ADA  ILE   HESTER
   ALISTAIRCOOK
UHURA  SINN   ROPE
MUSIC  AGOG   AGED
AREAS  YENS   PEN
```

36

```
T R I P   A R A B I A   O R B
H E N S   F A V O R S   N O R
E L W Y N B R O O K S   T S E
D E I C E   A N T I   S H E D
A T T H A T     I N O N E
    H E R B E R T G E O R G E
      S A T E     R O U E S
I A M B   R E L I T   K N O T
T I E I N     A R I A
A L A N A L E X A N D E R
  L E N I N     A D R E A M
J E T T   N E S T   E R A T O
A L I   J E R O M E D A V I D
K L M   E A G L E S   T O M E
E E E   T R Y O N S   A W E S
```

37

```
T O R E   A R B O R   S A N S
A P E S   D I A N A   C L A P
B E S T W I S H E S   A L M A
O R E   O D E S   C A L M E R
O A T B R A N   C A G E Y
    E M S   C O L E S L A W
C A S A S   G A Y L E   O L E
A R I D   C O N E Y   I V A N
P E N   G A T O R   B R E S T
P A C K I T I N   P E A
  E I G H T   H U G S A N D
P E R S I A   S A R A   Z O O
A L E S   Y O U R S T R U L Y
R I L E   A D I E U   O R A L
K E Y S   N O T M E   B E N E
```

38

```
A D E P T   S T O A S   A L B
R O M E O   H E A R T   Z O O
C L I N T W A L K E R   T U X
H E R N I A   L E N A   E S E
    I N D I A N A P A C E R
S T E   G E M   S P A
H U E S   D A N A   E R R O L
I N L A W   G A L   D O O N E
P A S H A   E G O S   N O T E
    I T S   F I R   F O R
G L O B E T R O T T E R
L A X   R E E L   A T E A S E
A M I   B L A D E R U N N E R
Z E D   E L C I D   R E T R O
E R E   D A T E S   N E S T S
```

39

```
E B B E D   I K E S   S C A T
A L I B I   L O F T   H O U R
R A Z O R S E D G E   O R G Y
T H E N   A A A   L E E R
H S T   N I C K E L O D E O N
    T I L   R A N   C R I
A W F U L   W O N T   S T A N
B A R B E R O F S E V I L L E
A S E A   E R A T   A B Y S S
S T E   O A T   H I S
H E L E N S H A V E R   T A M
  A V E S   C I A   F I X E
D R N O   I N H O T W A T E R
D E C K   G A E L   I M A L L
E P E E   N E S S   T E N S E
```

40

```
A N O N   S A L T   S W I S S
L E N O   W E A R   P A S T A
T H E G O O D H U M O R M A N
O R O   D O E R   A I D E R S
S U N L E S S   P Y L E
  A S H   G L A S N O S T
I T E M S   I R O N   L I E
T H E B A D N E W S B E A R S
C O L   R A G S   A B Y S S
H U S T L I N G   B I B
  H A V E   A L L S T A R
A S H O R E   F R E E   A B E
T H E U G L Y A M E R I C A N
N O R G E   A C E D   T E T E
O P A H S   W E D S   S T E W
```

```
O L A N D █ Q E D █ B A J E R
B O R E R █ U S A █ E N E M Y
J U M B O J E T S █ A D A T E
█ █ █ G A E A █ S T E N █ █ █
S O J O U R N █ V I S A V I S
A C U T E S █ M A R I N A D E
S E M I S █ C A P E T █ L E A
S A P S █ J A S O N █ A J A B
I N I █ S E N O R █ C R E T E
E I N S T E I N █ T O G A E D
R A G T O P S █ S E C O N D S
█ J U G S █ P E N H █ █ █ █
A B A C I █ J O L T I N J O E
B O C C E █ R P M █ S H E I K
M A K O S █ S E A █ E L U D E
```

```
L O C A L █ L A I R █ C R A M
O H A R A █ E I N E █ L A V A
T O R I C █ G R A B █ A C I D
T H R E E D A Y P A S S E S █
█ █ █ S U I T █ E T E S █ █ █
S A P █ P R I N T E R █ P A M
A R E A █ G O O █ V I R G O
T U R N S E N D O V E R E N D
U B O A T █ E V A █ A G E E
P A N █ O U R S E L F █ O W L
█ █ █ F I N E █ R E E D █ █ █
█ B L O C K A N D T A C K L E
P O O L █ E R O O █ S L I E R
I D O L █ P E N N █ T I L E R
N Y N Y █ T R E E █ S I L K S
```

```
I M A N █ A B L E █ A L L A H
R E N O █ P A I X █ L O I R E
A N T S █ I L S A █ L U M P Y
Q U I E T A S A M O U S E █
█ █ █ E R A █ P R Y █ █ █
P A S T R Y █ R A T E █ N O W
A F T E R █ M A G I █ T O P O
C O O L A S A C U C U M B E R
T O R E █ C R E E █ T E L L S
S T Y █ C H E R █ F I N E S T
█ █ S A M █ █ M A C █ █ █
█ S T R O N G A S A R O C K
A L L O T █ A U N T █ O P I E
S E I N E █ S A S E █ M A A M
P I P E R █ A M E R █ P L O P
```

```
A F R O █ S T A R R █ A B B A
S L E D █ L E V E E █ L A I R
H E A D T O H E A D █ M C L I
E E L █ A P E R █ E V O K E D
█ █ █ E P E E █ B E A S T █
A L F R E D █ S E M I T O N E
M E A N S █ H O V E L █ B I N
I N C A █ S A N E R █ T A C T
S T E █ R I V A L █ C A C H E
H O T C I D E R █ H A N K E R
█ █ O A T E S █ B A R K █ █
R I F L E S █ G A L L █ T A E
S L A M █ H A N D T O H A N D
V I C E █ O S A G E █ O B O E
P E E R █ W A T E R █ G U N N
```

```
W A D S █ O K R A █ C O R P S
H I R E █ W E I R █ O P E R A
I R E A L L Y D I D N T S A Y
S L A T E █ S E E R █ S O I L
K I M O N O █ █ S A G █ U S E
E N O █ A L S O █ B A R N E S
R E N D █ E A R P █ R E D D
█ █ █ Y O G I B E R R A █ █
█ A J A R █ L I T A █ R A M S
O R A N G E █ T E N K █ N A P
F R Y █ Y A M █ D I P O L E
F I L E █ S A R A █ W O M A N
E V E R Y T H I N G I S A I D
R A N G E █ E L K O █ E L S E
S L O O P █ R E A D █ D Y E R
```

46

```
L E A P   A T T I C   B A B A
I T E R   C H I N O   E M I R
A C R E   H E L L O   A I R E
R H O D E I S L A N D R E D S
    A L E E     S O U
H A T T E R   B I K E P A T H
A P R O N   S E M I   L O Y
F L O R I D A S U N S H I N E
T E L   I S T S   C O N A N
S A L T I N E S   P A M E L A
    U N O   R O L E
T E N N E S S E E W A L K E R
R Y A N   A I S L E   A N T I
A R N E   U P P E R   N E A P
M E A L   R E S T S   D E L E
```

47

```
B E T A   H A C K   C A C T I
A M A S   O B I E   O C H E R
R E B A   L O S E   S T O R E
C R O P C I R C L E S   P I S
A G O   A S T O   L A M S
R E S O R T   A L C O H O L
      N A I L E D   K R O N E
P A C T   C U T I N   A P E D
E L L A S   V E N O M S
S L I P U P S   B A S T E R
    P E P E   S P O T   R A E
E N C   P R U N E D A N I S H
V A L S E   L A N I   E S T E
I N O U R   N I N E   S H E A
L O P E S   A L E S   T A R T
```

48

```
A D A M   C A B A L   F E A T
M E G A   E L O P E   R E N O
O P E N I N G P R E S E N T S
S T R I C T   S O R E E Y E S
    C A R P   N E A R
B A S   R I A S   D R E W U P
U S E   U S L T A   I O T A
C H R I S T M A S D I N N E R
K E G S   S I T E S   T R I
O N E A C T   D E V O   S O S
    B A I L   R I G A
I N S E R T E D   L O C A T E
T O A L L A G O O D N I G H T
E V I L   N U E V O   D E A N
M A L A   S P R I G   S E T A
```

49

```
L A T H E   A R O M A   B A S
A R I E L   D O R A L   R N A
D R O P T H E B A L L   E A T
      R O L E     S W A M I
A P P E A S E   R E T A K E N
M E A N I E   H O B A R T
O R S O N   T A T A R   H B O
R O S S   B A R O N   B E A N
E N T   G A P E R   B R I C E
    H A R L E M   B E A C O N
A T E L I E R   B A R T E N D
L O B E S     B A T S
E M U   T A K E T H E C A K E
R E C   L I E T O   R U N A T
T S K   E D G A R   K E N Y A
```

50

```
J A M S   M E A R A   A G R I
O N E L   E T H E L   B L O B
B E G I N T H E B E G U I N E
S W A M I   M I X E D B A G
      E M I L   D I N H
S A G   I N I T   S T A T E N
E G O   T R O I S   B A D E
W A L T Z I N G M A T I L D A
E V E R   S E E N O   K I T
R E M I S S   R A K E   Y E S
      A N T E   R A C K
A F F L U E N T     A N G S T
B E E R B A R R E L P O L K A
B E A U   L O E W E   L E I F
A T T N   S L E E T   L E N T
```

51

H	B	O	M	B		G	A	I	T		H	A	R	K
A	R	N	I	E		O	R	C	A		E	T	U	I
H	E	A	D	H	U	N	T	E	R		D	O	L	L
A	W	N		O	R	G	Y		P	I	G	P	E	N
			H	O	G	S		S	A	M	E			
A	L	C	O	V	E		S	A	P	P	H	I	R	E
V	A	L	U	E		M	I	L	E		O	D	E	S
A	D	E	S		S	O	L	A	R		P	E	A	T
S	L	O	E		Q	U	A	D		S	P	A	D	E
T	E	N	H	O	U	R	S		R	E	E	S	E	S
			O	L	I	N		A	U	E	R			
E	A	G	L	E	S		A	C	T	S		E	S	P
S	L	I	D		H	I	G	H	H	A	T	T	E	R
P	O	L	E		E	R	I	E		W	H	A	L	E
N	E	A	R		D	E	N	S		S	U	L	L	Y

52

T	A	C	O	S		D	O	R	M		U	M	P	S
A	L	E	P	H		A	D	E	E		T	I	L	E
R	O	D	E	O		M	O	A	N		O	L	I	N
T	H	E	C	O	L	O	R	P	U	R	P	L	E	
S	A	D		E	O	N			I	I	I			
			O	D	S		I	C	E	P	A	C	K	S
S	L	A	Y		E	R	A	S	E		E	E	E	
W	I	L	L	I	A	M	O	F	O	R	A	N	G	E
I	S	M		C	L	I	N	E		I	T	S	A	
M	I	S	D	I	A	L	S		W	A	R			
			H	E	N		C	A	N		A	C	T	
	L	O	N	G	J	O	H	N	S	I	L	V	E	R
L	O	U	T		O	R	E	O		M	O	I	R	E
A	P	S	E		C	A	R	T		A	R	L	E	N
W	E	E	D		K	N	E	E		L	E	A	S	T

53

H	O	R	N	S		A	C	T		L	A	T	T	E
A	B	O	U	T		L	O	O		A	M	I	E	S
H	O	W	T	O	W	I	N	F	R	I	E	N	D	S
A	E	S		O	R	T		F	O	R	B	A	D	E
			A	L	I	A	S	E	S		A	T	E	N
B	O	C	A		N	L	W	E	S	T		U	R	E
C	A	R	N	E	G	I	E		I	G	O	R		
D	R	E	D	D		A	N	D		I	O	N	I	A
		A	P	E	G		S	E	L	F	H	E	L	P
F	A	M		N	I	C	O	L	E		E	R	L	E
A	L	P	E		J	A	N	I	T	O	R			
C	O	U	N	T	O	N		M	U	D		S	A	L
I	N	F	L	U	E	N	C	E	P	E	O	P	L	E
A	S	F	A	R		E	P	A		T	W	A	I	N
L	O	S	I	N		S	A	T		S	E	T	T	O

54

S	E	I	Z	E		S	L	A	T		A	B	L	E
P	A	C	E	R		H	E	R	R		V	O	I	D
A	R	E	N	A		O	N	C	E		A	N	T	I
			S	A	W	T	H	E	L	I	G	H	T	
L	A	P	P	E	R			A	L	O	E	S		
A	R	L	O		M	U	S	K	E	T				
T	R	U	E	S		S	T	O	N	E		H	A	S
H	A	M	M	E	R	H	E	A	D	S	H	A	R	K
E	Y	E		Q	U	E	L	L		T	O	N	G	A
			U	N	R	E	A	L		R	O	O	T	
A	G	A	P	E			I	G	N	I	T	E		
D	R	I	L	L	M	A	S	T	E	R				
M	A	D	E		A	V	E	R		E	A	S	E	L
I	D	E	A		C	O	M	A		E	L	I	T	E
T	E	S	T		S	W	I	M		D	I	S	C	O

55

T	A	P	S		C	L	A	I	M		D	R	A	B
A	H	O	Y		H	A	N	N	A		H	I	K	E
N	A	I	L	B	I	T	I	N	G		A	B	R	I
		L	O	R	E	N		N	O	R	T	O	N	
S	A	H	A	R	A	N		D	O	O	M	I	N	G
A	R	A	B	I	C		B	A	L	Z	A	C		
V	E	I	L	S		G	E	N	I	E		K	G	B
E	T	R	E		H	E	N	N	A		S	L	O	E
D	E	R		B	A	N	D	Y		S	T	I	R	S
		A	I	R	B	U	S		S	W	A	N	E	E
P	H	I	D	I	A	S		A	M	O	N	G	S	T
L	E	S	I	O	N		B	L	O	O	D			
O	L	I	O		E	Y	E	P	O	P	P	I	N	G
P	I	N	T		R	E	L	E	T		A	R	I	A
S	O	G	S		A	W	A	S	H		T	E	X	T

56

```
S W A L E   O S H A   A T L
S O M E R S   A W E S   R I A
W O M E N L I K E S I L E N T
  D O R S E T   E S S E N C E
M T N   D E B T   F A U N
P R I M P   M A P S   T S P S
S I T O U T   B E A S T
  M E N T H E Y A S S U M E
  A T O M S   S T R O N G
P A R R   R E A L   S N I T S
A L E C   R T E S   E R A
T O S H I B A   S O N A T A
T H E Y R E L I S T E N I N G
I A N   O L D S   S E N E C A
E S T   N A S T   D O S E S
```

57

```
C Z A R   S W I L L   C L A D
I O W A   K O R E A   L E N O
A N O N   I R A N I   O M E N
  E L D E R S T A T E S M A N
    A C U T E   L E A R Y
A V A L O N   E R A T
G I L L   A U T O N O M I C
O N A   O L D M A I D   I V E
G O R E V I D A L   S C A N
    Q U E S   D E C E N T
S E O U L   A M U L E
A N C I E N T M A R I N E R
I T O N   O R A T E   E L A N
N E M O   N A Z I S   R I C O
T R E X   O P E N S   Y A K S
```

58

```
M A R S   M A M A   K A R A N
A B U T   I C O N   O M E G A
R O S E   T R O Y   W I D E R
I U S E D T O   T E D D Y
S T O R E   S A Y S O
  B E S N O W W H I T E
S L I D I N   D N A   O D E R
L U N E T S   T A L E N T
A L A S   U S A   H U M A N E
B U T I D R I F T E D
  R E C T O   I O N I A
R A I S A   M A E W E S T
A S K E W   L A M B   N A N O
S T E R E   E V I L   E T O N
P O S E R   S E X Y   R O T E
```

59

```
  D E C A L   R E L O   A W S
D E L U D E   A T O M   D I M
O C E L O T   S H O E T R E E
F L A T B U S H   G E E N A
F A N   E P A   S C A N N E R
E R O S   P A T H   D A R E
D E R A T S   S E E P   L S D
  C H I C K W E E D
D I D   E R I E   P R E S E T
I F A T   E N D S   T H R O
C O M R A D E   T A O   E O S
K R A I T   E E L G R A S S
E G G P L A N T   F L U T I E
N E E   A R E A   R E S H O D
S T S   S E W S   E S S E N
```

60

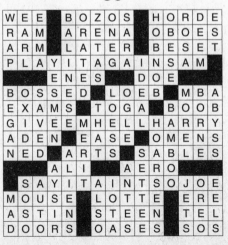

```
W E E   B O Z O S   H O R D E
R A M   A R E N A   O B O E S
A R M   L A T E R   B E S E T
P L A Y I T A G A I N S A M
    E N E S   D O E
B O S S E D   L O E B   M B A
E X A M S   T O G A   B O O B
G I V E E M H E L L H A R R Y
A D E N   E A S E   O M E N S
N E D   A R T S   S A B L E S
    A L I   A E R O
S A Y I T A I N T S O J O E
M O U S E   L O T T E   E R E
A S T I N   S T E E N   T E L
D O O R S   O A S E S   S O S
```

61

A	N	W	A	R		S	C	R	A	M		A	R	C
N	O	O	S	E		H	O	Y	L	E		W	A	R
T	U	E	S	D	A	Y	W	E	L	D		A	D	O
I	N	S	T	A	L	L	S		T	I	A	R	A	S
			L	A	Y		W	H	A	L	E	R	S	
A	W	A	K	E	N		I	R	E	N	E			
C	A	G	E	R		A	V	E	R			D	A	S
T	W	E	N	T	Y	N	I	N	E	P	A	L	M	S
S	A	D			U	T	E	S		E	L	I	O	T
			A	C	M	E	S		B	A	T	I	K	S
M	O	S	L	E	M	S		S	E	C				
A	L	K	A	L	I		S	W	E	E	T	E	S	T
V	I	E		L	E	A	P	O	F	F	A	I	T	H
E	V	E		O	S	C	A	R		U	L	N	A	E
N	E	T		S	T	E	R	N		L	E	E	R	Y

62

T	H	A	T		G	R	I	N	S		E	L	S	E
H	E	R	A		E	A	S	E	D		S	O	M	E
E	L	M	S		T	I	S	H	A		T	S	A	R
W	E	A	K	I	N	T	H	E	K	N	E	E	S	
A	N	D		T	O	T	E	M		O	R	T	H	O
Y	E	A	R	S			I	A	N			I	U	D
			E	M	T		H	A	D	J		M	P	S
	E	A	S	Y	O	N	T	H	E	E	Y	E	S	
P	V	C		T	R	I	S		E	W	E			
T	I	E		U	N	C				I	N	F	O	R
A	L	T	A	R		O	U	S	T	S		R	N	A
	D	O	W	N	A	T	T	H	E	H	E	E	L	S
B	O	N	A		R	I	T	E	S		C	R	I	P
R	E	E	K		K	N	E	L	T		R	E	N	E
O	R	S	E		S	E	R	F	S		U	S	E	D

63

T	H	E	M		S	A	S	S		C	D	R	O	M
H	O	P	E		E	S	T	A		A	R	O	M	A
U	N	I	T		T	H	A	N		T	A	M	E	R
S	E	C	R	E	T	A	G	E	N	T	M	A	N	
			O	N	E	R			O	L	A			
M	A	J		D	E	P	E	C	H	E		A	S	H
E	L	I	H	U		A	S	I		A	L	T	O	
S	E	M	I	P	R	I	V	A	T	E	R	O	O	M
A	R	M	S		U	K	E		A	T	O	N	E	
S	T	Y		K	N	E	S	S	E	T		F	E	D
			S	N	O			I	V	E	S			
	L	A	C	O	N	F	I	D	E	N	T	I	A	L
H	A	S	A	T		A	G	I	N		U	S	N	A
S	T	I	N	T		T	O	N	S		F	E	N	D
T	E	S	T	Y		E	R	G	O		F	E	E	S

64

A	C	R	E		C	R	I	E	R		C	A	M	P
R	A	I	N		L	O	O	S	E		A	R	I	A
O	F	F	T	H	E	O	U	T	S		S	A	L	T
M	E	T		A	R	T	S		T	R	I	B	E	S
A	S	S	I	S	I			C	A	A	N			
			O	N	C	O	L	O	R	J	O	K	E	S
P	A	I	N	T		H	A	S	T	A		I	L	E
A	M	P	S		D	E	R	M	S		S	N	I	T
L	E	S		F	U	N	G	I		S	O	D	A	S
O	N	O	N	E	S	R	O	C	K	E	R			
			A	T	T	Y			O	T	T	E	R	S
B	A	L	S	A	M		O	S	S	A		M	A	E
A	D	O	S		O	F	F	T	H	E	M	E	N	D
L	E	S	E		P	E	A	L	E		U	R	G	E
L	E	E	R		S	E	N	O	R		D	Y	E	R

65

F	A	L	S	E		A	L	O	H	A		S	R	S
E	L	E	C	T		P	A	T	O	N		T	I	N
I	S	A	A	C	N	E	W	T	O	N		E	G	O
N	O	R	M		O	R	L	O	P		A	V	O	W
			P	A	U	S	E		L	I	T	E	R	S
B	A	A	I	N	G		S	T	A	M	E	N		
L	T	D		D	A	I	S	Y		M	A	J	O	R
E	M	A	N	A	T	E		P	R	O	M	O	T	E
W	O	M	A	N		S	N	E	E	R		B	O	A
			A	S	T	U	T	E		T	A	S	S	E	L
C	E	N	T	E	R		S	W	I	L	L			
L	A	D	Y		S	A	T	A	N		A	M	O	S
A	R	E		W	I	L	L	I	A	M	T	E	L	L
M	T	V		A	N	D	E	S		C	E	L	L	O
S	H	E		Y	E	A	S	T		I	D	T	A	G

66

```
C E L E B   A D O     P A P A
A L E V E   J E W   M O N A D
S U G A R C A N E   U R G E D
E D U   L U X E   A S T R A L
R E P A I R   B I S C A Y N E
      S O S O   T I L L
C I T I Z E N K A N E   T A J
A D E S   S O L   A E R O
B O X   R A I S I N G C A I N
    A I N T   C A R E
H E R B C A E N   C O R A L S
A M U L E T   O A H U   B A T
N I N E R   N O V O C A I N E
G L O S S   A N O   H I N G E
S E N T   P E W   O R D E R
```

67

```
G R A S S   P L O   S M O K E
S I N A I   L A C   E I D E R
A D D L E   A T T E N D I N G
    M R S T H E P O I N T
S A T I R E   S T I R
E T H   A V E   S C I S S O R
A T E   E L M   T I L D E
M I S S I N F O R M A T I O N
A L I E N   P I E   E N D
N A S T I E R   P C B   S T E
    T A O S   C A P T O R
M R B I R T H D A Y S
N E U R A L G I A   O A R E D
A R I E L   U R N   U L T R A
G E N T S   T E A   S M E A R
```

68

```
S P A R K Y   S E S   G A M
T I T H E D   C H A W   O R E
E A T E R S   H E R A   O T T
A N I O N   S A L L Y   D I E
D O C   E N T R   Y E A G E R
    B L U E L Y   R R R
I T S O   K I E V   S T I P E
S A C S   E N S O R   F E L L
H O H U M   E S N E   U F O S
    R N A   M C N E I L
G H O S T S   H E L M   P A S
R A E   L I N U S   S M A L L
A N D   E T A L   S U B T L E
D O E   S I T Z   P R A T E D
S I R   S N O   Y E S Y E S
```

69

```
O S H A   A B O M B   M A M A
A L E C   T I B E R   O M E N
R O A R   O P E R A   B O A T
  B R O W N E Y E D G I R L
    S H E D   S A L
H A S T A   S A M   S E L M A
A T T I C S   L O U   L A I
B L A C K E Y E D S U S A N S
L A B   X I V   E N A M E L
A S S E T   N E W   T R A D E
    Y A K   H A I G
  G R E E N E Y E D L A D Y
B O I L   O L A N D   S E E P
O N C E   W I N C E   S E A L
B E E T   N A K E D   O P R Y
```

70

```
A M P S   D U O S   S T A S H
M A I L   A N N E   C A R T E
E D D A   D I E M   O X B O W
B E G T H E Q U E S T I O N
A D I E U   U P S E T   R E D
S O N   M A E   T E Y   E A R
    D O S   E E K   B A G S
  B O R R O W T R O U B L E
D A V Y   C O S   U M S
E N E   S I R   S T P   S P A
F I R   T A S S O   E A T I T
  S T E A L T H I R D B A S E
A T I L T   O I L Y   O R C A
F E M M E   F R E E   V E E S
T R E S S   F E D S   E S S E
```

71

```
DOOR   PRIM  TAMPA
ALSO   LENO  ONEAL
MALT   ASTO  STAID
EVOCATION    TINGE
     LES   TASTER
SCOPE  THIRD
ALLIES EQUALITY
FADE   MIDST  AROO
EMERGING     HAZARD
     ARNEL  PENTA
REMARK    OSO
ALARM  EQUIPPING
JESSE  RUNT   AVON
ANTON  MAGI   RAGA
HASNT  ADEN   KNOW
```

72

```
PADS   PRISM  WEDS
LION   HARTE  ITAL
ARNO   ONEAT  SUMO
ZEN    OTISREDDING
ADAGIO     TORO
     FOLSOM  RAMJET
OPALS  DENIM   ORO
LORD   SONIC  SHAM
DOG    AURAL  SENSE
SHOGUN    TESTED
     ODDS    MUSEUM
PATTIAUSTIN    NBA
ALUM   NEPAL  AVON
LIRA   CRATE  TEAS
LAND   ESSES  ARTE
```

73

```
LSAT   PIAF   EFLAT
ACTA   OLLA   QUOTH
TABCOLLAR     UNCLE
ELAINE NIPAT
LATTICE NAB    APE
YRS  CABCALLOWAY
     METRO  LESAGE
SPAY   ONA    LYES
COHOST ANGLO
ARABCOUNTRY   FIR
REB    HEN  SARDINE
     AUDIO  BIERCE
ATALL  CRABCAKES
RELIT  EAVE   RISE
BLITZ  FLED   ENTS
```

74

```
ADOS   ESP    USABLE
RUTH   ATE    SCREEN
ROBINSON      SHINED
     NOTING  MDCCI
RBI    SEC  ERI   HHS
YASSER   THEDA
ALLCENTURYTEAM
NEER   ARI    ODAS
  STARTINGLINEUP
     MAILS  ONSALE
SSS    TOO  OCT  LSD
OPERA  RIPKEN
COGITO   WILLIAMS
KOUFAX ANE    MAYS
SLEETY SET    SHOT
```

75

```
SWAB   DIMES  KAYE
OHNO   EVENT  AWAY
WOOF   CARLA  PEKE
SANFRANCISCO
     OAR   SHOWOFF
ARC   FLOUTED  REL
BOYSTOWN   SANDRA
ACNE   NBA    BERM
SKIERS ADAMSRIB
ENC   ETAGERE  SSE
DESKSET   MAC
  SPENCERTRACY
JOLT   POOLE  OUZO
AREA   LOPES  CRAW
BEAR   ENACT  KARL
```

The New York Times

Crossword Puzzles

The #1 name in crosswords

Available at your local bookstore or online at nytimes.com/nytstore

St. Martin's Griffin